UNDERSTANDING THE FILIPINO

UNDERSTANDING THE FILIPINO

Tomas D. Andres

Pilar Corazon B. Ilada-Andres

NEW DAY PUBLISHERS
Quezon City, Philippines
1987

Published by
New Day Publishers
11 Lands St., Project 6, Quezon City
P. O. Box 167, Quezon City 3008
Philippines
Tel. 99-80-46

Cover design by Achilles B. Mina

ISBN 971-10-0337-6

To our six precious jewels

THOMAS PHILAMER
PILAR PHILAMER
PIERREANGELO PHILAMER
LORD PHILAMER
PATRICIAN PHILAMER
BERNARD PHILAMER

and all the other children and young people
of the world, in the hope that the new generation
will grow in mutual love and respect
for each other's cultures.

Other Books by the Author
Published by New Day Publishers

Understanding Values (1980)

Human Resource Training and Development (1980)

Understanding Filipino Values: A Management Approach (1981)

Organizational Development for Productivity in the Philippine
  Setting (1983)

Management by Filipino Values (1985)

Organizing a Training Program — A Manual (1986)

PREFACE

To a foreigner, living in the Philippine culture is like playing a game one has never played before and of which the rules haven't been explained very well. This book aims to provide the reader with an understanding of the "game" and some of its rules. The challenge, however, is for the reader to enjoy the game without missing the joys and fun of living in the Philippines.

This book is a detailed study of Filipino etiquette, values, mores, customs and manners which show the differences as well as similarities in behavioral expectations that arise when a Westerner comes to live in an Eastern culture. Filipinos often think, sometimes with good cause, that Westerners are rude and make no attempt to adapt themselves to the manners and customs of their host country. However, when one is ignorant of the fact that such rules exist he can hardly be blamed for not conforming to them. Hence, this book.

A stranger or foreigner who has a knowledge of the Filipino society's customs, etiquette, and manners, is less likely to experience intense culture shock. Hopefully, this book will lead to a better understanding and appreciation of the Philippines as a host country and help every visitor in this country to settle in a more comfortable way and eventually enjoy mutual beneficial social, personal and business relationships.

Tomas D. Andres
Pilar Corazon B. Ilada-Andres
Values and Technologies
  Management Centre
Sta. Mesa, Manila

ACKNOWLEDGMENTS

Many people helped shape and complete this work. Authorities in the field of anthropology, sociology, psychology and Philippine culture and other related disciplines as well as practitioners shared their insights with the writers and their contributions are deeply acknowledged. In the preparation of this work, therefore, the writers wish to give due recognition to the following:

Expatriates we have interviewed and dealt with in multinational and international organizations: Yolanda del Mundo, Nancy V. Paje and Tessie Tiapolet of the Philippine Tourism Authority; Mr. Freddie E. Jimenez and Ms. Cholly Coronado of Aris (Philippines), Inc.; the Canadian Executive Services Organization of the Philippines; Angelina B. Ilada, Marie Nancy Ortiz, Perla Ilada, Marcelina Duldulao, Nicholle Donato and hundreds of Filipinos who shared with us their knowledge of customs, superstitions and beliefs of Filipinos, students and fellow professors of Ateneo de Manila University, De La Salle University, Dr. Conchita Largoza and other personnel managers of the Personnel Management Association of the Philippines; Human Resources Managers of the Philippine Society for Training and Development; Toyota, Filipinas Dravo, and CDCP from whom we gathered a lot of insights regarding expatriates' life; our elder brothers Mr. Jose D. Andres of King Wilkinson (SA) Ltd. and Engr. Bernardino D. Andres, Jr. of General Motors, whose overseas experiences in Saudi Arabia and Brazil, respectively, have enriched this book; Ms. Antoinette de Castro-Bonifacio of the Visa Section of the American Embassy in the Philippines; Ms. Josefina de Castro-Zita of Security Bank and Trust Company; and the staff of the Central Bank Institute, University of Life, Ministry of Education, Culture and Sports and Ministry of Labor and Employment; Ms. Gloria F. Rodriguez and Ms. Elayda C. Marasigan of *New Day Publishers*.

As the saying goes, "There's nothing new under the sun." We fully acknowledge that what we have written here have been taken from other sources and experiences and from our lectures, briefings, and personal teaching notes. As much as we can we acknowledge all the references used in the bibliography; however, human frailty dictates that some authors or sources may not have been acknowledged or mentioned explicitly due to inadvertence or lack of documentation. To them we give due thanks and acknowledgment.

Last but not least, our thanks and gratitude go to our loving children, Thomas Philamer, Pilar Philamer, Pierreangelo Philamer, Lord Philamer, Patrician Philamer and Bernard Philamer for their cooperation and inspiration.

THE AUTHORS

CONTENTS

xii

PART ONE

AN ORIENTATION ON FILIPINO CULTURE

1 UNDERSTANDING FILIPINO CULTURE

WELCOME TO THE PHILIPPINES! Welcome to this country of warm smiles and vivacious people! Getting to know the Filipinos is easy enough. If you speak English, you'll find that most of them speak the language; and what's more, they are only too happy to make your acquaintance in English. Even if you don't, the Filipino is so outgoing by nature that making friends out of total strangers or chance acquaintances is simply being in character. However, to be effective in your mission or enjoy your stay in the Philippines, you need to know thoroughly the Filipino: his values, his idiosyncrasies, his psychological make-up.

The Filipinos are a happy blend of several races, basically Malay with Chinese, Spanish, Indian and American admixtures. Their values and ways of life were shaped by several, sometimes conflicting cultures and the resulting blend is what makes their own uniquely Filipino. In their veins run the rich Christian values of Europe, the pragmatic and democratic values of America, and the spiritual values of Asia. Thus, these differences must be known to you to avoid stress and anxiety.

There are innumerable differences between Filipinos and Westerners. What is important is for a foreigner to adjust and understand the Filipino. He must have one foot in the Filipino culture and the other in his own. He has to study and understand the inner logic and coherence of the Filipino culture to appreciate it. While retaining his own value system, he expands his attitude and etiquette to include those of the Filipinos' in the name of friendship and goodwill. He needs empathy, curiosity, interest and acceptance of the cultural differences. He must be inquisitive, docile and willing to learn from the Filipino people. Without losing his high self-concept, he can be humble and have respect for the Filipinos and their values.

The Filipino Culture

Filipino culture is an integrated system of learned behavior patterns that are characteristic of the members of the Philippine society. It refers to the total way of life of the Filipinos. It includes everything that the Filipinos think, say, do or make. It includes Philippine customs, traditions, language, values, beliefs, attitudes, concepts of self, morals, rituals and manners.

The Filipino culture, like any other culture, grew differently because of its need to respond to Filipino problems. A foreigner coming to or staying in the Philippines must know two important points regarding culture; *first*, it is important that he accepts that there are no intrinsically "right" or "wrong" solutions, no objectively "better" or "worse" ways of meeting basic needs; *secondly*, every culture is and has always been ethnocentric, that is, it thinks its own solutions are superior and would be recognized as superior by any "right-thinking," intelligent, logical human being.

The Filipino and the foreigner who come from varied cultural backgrounds see the same objects and situations differently. For the Westerner, for example, to eat with bare hands is "dirty"; for the Filipino, it is the usual thing to do. It will be impossible for the foreigner to understand what the actions of the Filipino mean if he analyzes them in terms of his own motives and values; he must interpret the Filipino behavior in the light of Filipino motives, habits, and values. The same behavior has different meanings in his culture and in the Filipino culture, and he must look at the Filipino behavior in relation to the culture of the Philippine society in which it takes place. In short the meaning of Filipino behavior is related to the Filipino culture in which it occurs.

The Filipino culture is not only the physical geography that takes in the land, the climate, physical and natural resources; it includes the human geography that takes in the people, the demography, tribes, migrations, locations, language; the institutions of the culture which includes the customs, the rituals, the

4

ceremonies and beliefs. It also encompasses the historical density of the Filipino culture, the cultural density, and the collective experience of the Filipino people. This means the history of the Filipinos, the whole cultural heritage built up through generations which comprise the "truths by which Filipinos live," the collective experience which has brought the Filipinos successfully this far and which are shared almost unconsciously.

The seven distinct elements in Filipino culture are values, basic personality, basic social unit, politics, economics, technology and ecology. Each of these aspects of the Filipino culture has a body of ideas called "content" which gives form and meaning to each aspect. This form and meaning are expressed through "structures" or institutions which the Philippine society creates for the orderly regulation of behavior in established ways.

Filipino cultural values are widely-held beliefs which make some activities, relationships, goals and feelings important to the Filipino people's identity. When these Filipino values coalesce and mesh in a mutually supportive system, it is called Filipino value system. The content of the Filipino values are the Filipino myths and religion while the structures are the Filipino oral and written traditions, churches, sacred places, temples and mosques. The Filipinos internalize these values of their culture and thus create for themselves "a world of meanings."

The Filipino basic personality is determined by the Filipino culture because of the selection of those congruent types that are congruent with the culture. The content of the Filipino basic personality is made up of Filipino beliefs and knowledge while the structure is formed by the Filipino initiation and various rituals and formal and informal education.

The Filipino basic social unit is the family which contributes to and maintains the Filipino values. The content of the Filipino social unit is the family, groups and community life while the structure is the lineage, marriage descent, neighborhood, peer group and villages.

The Filipino politics are the Filipino ideas and structures related to the distribution and channeling of power within the Philippine society for its well-being, order and regulation. The content of politics is the Filipino traditional power units and democracy while the structures are the rule of law, parliament, councils, elders and chiefs.

The Filipino economics are the ideas which the Philippine

5

society develops and the structures which it creates for provision of food, clothing and shelter for its members. The content of Philippine economics is the production by private enterprises while its structure is capitalism and socialism.

Filipino technology includes all that the Filipinos have invented to make their life easier, less arduous, and shifted from the brink of mere survival thus changing their way of life and giving them more control of their physical environment. Its contents are communication and health while its structure is composed of the various media, professional organizations, medicine, hospitals and laboratories.

Filipino ecology is the relation of the Filipino to the ecosystem such as temperature, type of soil, amount of moisture, types of crops that can be grown or types of animals present in the Philippines and other environmental features. The content of Filipino ecology is the identification of the Filipino with nature and its structure include hunting, fishing, nature worship and irrigation.

Cultural Contrasts

The Filipino, compared with Westerners, prefers a "structured" way of life rather than one in which he can be assertive of his own individuality. Thus a Westerner will find the Filipino less autonomous and more dependent. This is because of the social concept of the Filipino self-esteem. His concept of self is identified with his family. Right from childhood he is made to believe that he belongs to the family. Since childhood a Filipino is encouraged to tell all of his thoughts to his parents and submit to his parents' direction, counsel and advice. He is admonished to be good because any disgrace that he commits is a disgrace to the family. In times of misfortune he is assured of his family's support, sympathy and love.

By Western standards, the Filipino parents can be considered overprotective and sometimes intrusive. However, if one understands this seemingly unreasonable control in the context of the Philippine culture wherein exists the belief in the primacy of the extended family over that of the individual and that the only source of emotional, economic, and moral support is the family, one will be more tolerant of such actuations.

In the Philippines, smooth interpersonal relationship (SIR) is the rule for any relationship. One must avoid showing signs of conflict when relating to a Filipino. As much as possible he must never show a sour look, nor utter harsh words. As much as possible he must never disagree openly. A smile, a friendly lift of the eyebrow, a pat on the back, a squeeze of the arm, a word of praise or a friendly concern can easily win the friendship of a Filipino. Filipinos compared with Westerners are more sensitive and easily humiliated. One must never ridicule a Filipino. He considers with a great deal of resentment a ridicule coming from a foreigner or stranger, though not so much from a fellow Filipino or townmate. According to Dr. Lourdes V. Lapuz, Filipinos less often kill family members than do Americans, but they more often kill strangers, again in situations in which momentary difficulties in interpersonal relations develop.[1] The Filipino is sensitive to hard words and aggressive behavior.

Another cultural trait of the Filipino is that he is a poor loser. He is unable to take defeat gracefully. If he wins, he is exceedingly jubilant; if he loses, he is exceedingly bitter. In athletics, he is deeply sportsminded but tends to be unsportsmanlike. To many Filipinos to be defeated is to be humiliated. Thus, the Filipino when he loses is apt to put up an excuse or alibi. A sociological explanation for this Filipino attitude towards defeat is the colonial and unfortunate experience suffered by them during the Spanish era during which they have always been relegated to the rank of inferiors. The phenomenon has made the Filipinos very sensitive as a people. Thus, for the Filipino, defeat is a sign of inferiority and subordination. An alibi or excuse when one loses is a defense mechanism against accepting the superiority and dominance of the winner.

Westerners tend to regulate their contact with Filipinos by failing to observe the gap; Filipinos tend to regulate their contact with Westerners by a clear recognition that differences exist and a shallow and incurious notion of what these consist of. Filipinos limit their contact with the Westerners in their midst partly by shifting to the Tagalog dialect, and by a variety of other defensive measures whereby they try, understandably, to evade the experience of difference.

It is impossible to understand what the actions of Filipinos mean if they are analyzed in terms of Western motives and values. Their behavior must be interpreted in the light of Filipino

7

motives, habits and values. Take the case of how death and funerals are handled in the Philippines. Western handling of death and funerals requires silence and stiff decorum, requires that the privacy of the bereaved be respected since they are supposed to want to be alone and includes a suspension of all references to the material facts of every day such as food and money. The Filipino way of handling death or to be exact *"paglalamay"* or "vigil" is exactly the opposite of the Western way. In the Philippines when a dead body laid out in a coffin is placed in the funeral parlor or in the family's house, the relatives gather, people come and go, express condolences and contribute money, stand by and gossip; young boys and girls play word games and flirt at the door; gambling tables and barbecues are set up around the house, with general merriment, singing and guitar-playing going on throughout the night.

Westerners' handling of bereavement requires that the bereaved person should not be reminded of what has happened, not be asked to talk about it. Tact requires that the name of the dead person be mentioned only with extreme circumspect, that the details be glossed over, and the emotions not rearoused. Filipino way of handling bereavement is exactly the opposite way. Filipinos would express sympathy and concern by asking specific factual questions and the primary assumption about those who have suffered a loss is that they should not be left alone. A Westerner should not be scandalized if a Filipino friend starts asking detailed facts about the dead such as "How did he die?", "Did he suffer much?", "How much did you spend at the hospital?" etc. This is the Filipino way of saying "We were so sorry to hear that your father died." He is just genuinely trying to express concern and affection.

The Catholic orientation of the Filipino makes him handle death and birth as ordinary familiar experiences while most Westerners treat grief with silence and repressed feelings. Thus, in their handling of death, Filipinos might be characterized by Westerners as "brutally frank" while Westerners may be characterized by Filipinos as euphemistic and indirect. The Filipino tolerance for the rhythms of life is deeply healing.

While there exists a degree of uniformity of Philippine culture throughout the country, there are still subcultural differences which affect the meaning of behavior and values. Take the case of urban nightclubs featuring "topless" entertainers as a deliberate type of sexual allurement. If a Westerner happens to go to the remote mountain districts of the Philippines, bare-breasted women go about their tasks with no thought of sexual suggestion but quickly run for cover when word spreads that lowlanders with a different cultural interpretation are in the vicinity. Similarly, if a lowland Filipino young man or young woman announces that he was through living with his parents and is going to live on his own, this would be taken as a sign of rebellion against parental authority. Among Bontocs, the practice of the young sleeping in separate buildings is a normal part of the behavior expected of conventional youth. This indicates that in a particular cultural setting, certain traits are right because they work in that setting, while other traits are wrong because they would clash painfully with some elements of the culture.

2 THE FILIPINO PROFILE

The Philippines is composed of 7,107 islands with a total land area of 296,912 square kilometers. This makes it a little larger than the British Isles and a little smaller than Japan. Its land area is eight times larger than Taiwan, 2/3 the size of either Thailand or Spain, but less than 1/30 of the size of the United States or Mainland China.

The country is bounded on the west by the China Sea, on the east by the Pacific Ocean, and on the south by the Celebes Sea. It lies a little above the equator and is 965 kilometers (600 miles) off the southeast coast of the Asian mainland. It is about 160 kilometers (100 miles) below Taiwan, and 24 kilometers above Borneo.

The Philippines has a population of 50 million Filipinos.[2] Its population growth rate has been estimated at 2.71 per annum over the period 1975–80. It has the highest growth rate in Asia. Its population density per square kilometer of non-forest land stands at 274.

The population of the country is rather unevenly distributed on the larger islands due to livelihood opportunities, social and economic organizations and historical factors. Its biggest islands are Luzon, Mindanao, Mindoro, Samar, Panay, Cebu, Palawan, Leyte, Bohol and Masbate. Its largest cities are Manila, Quezon City, Davao and Cebu.

The Philippine population is characterized by an almost equal number of males and females. The sex ratio of 100.7 observed in 1980 implies that there is but a very slight preponderance of males over the females in the population. Forty percent of

10

Filipinos are below 15 years of age. Literacy stands at 82.7 percent. Close to ten percent of the population seven years of age reportedly did not have any formal education.[3] Professionals constitute but a minority in Philippine society with less than five percent having received an academic degree.

The Philippines has for its languages Pilipino, English and Spanish; it has 87 different major dialects ranging from Tagalog, Sugbuanon, Hiligaynon, Samarnon, Bikol, Pampango, Ilocano, Maguindanao, Maranaw to Tausug. English is widely spoken; in fact, this country is the third largest English-speaking nation in the world.

Most Filipinos are rural people and farmers. There are many barrios dotting the countryside. Though there is a gradual shift from agriculture to non-agricultural activities, more than one half of male Filipino workers are still engaged in agriculture. The two pronounced seasons in the Philippines are the rainy months from June to October and the dry months from November to May. In between these seasons come a number of typhoons that hit the country yearly.

The principal products of the Philippines are rice, corn, coconut, sugar cane, bananas, tobacco. Its major products are processed agricultural products, textiles, chemicals and chemical products. Its natural resources are forests, metallic and non-metallic mines. Its exports are coconut products, sugar, logs and lumber, copper concentrates, bananas, nickel and garments.

Malay, Chinese and Indian Facets of the Filipino

The Filipino is predominantly of Malayan ancestry with Chinese culture as base. The Malay in the Filipino is manifested by his readiness to adjust to a new situation and his desire to be above all, nice. He presents a smiling countenance, makes seemingly decorous gestures, speaks cordial words that signify the delicacy of his feelings, is gracious and hospitable. To the predominantly Malay Filipino, frankness is a breach of courtesy, righteousness and eccentricity. Thus, he says nothing negative of anything that he does not approve of, not that it is wrong or that it is illegal, but that it is "ugly" (*pangit*) or "not nice." The best man for him is one who is "easy to get along with."

The Filipino culture is predominantly Chinese. Strongest

11

evidence lies in the Filipinos age-old manner of addressing their grandparents as *Lolo* and *Lola*, their brothers as *Kuya*, *Diko*, and their sisters as *Ate*, and *Diche*. The use of fans, slippers and umbrellas are of Chinese origin. The practice of using white clothes for mourning among the Moslem Filipinos today is undoubtedly of Chinese origin. The sleeved jackets and loose trousers of the Moslem women, the pajamas of the Christian Filipinos, and the barong Tagalog which is nationally popular as a male attire are of Chinese origin. Filipinos love to eat Chinese food such as *pansit*, *chopsuey*, *misua*, *siopao*, *lumpia*, and *lugaw*. Pansit and misua are varieties of Chinese noodles; chopsuey is a Chinese-Filipino dish with a mixture of different vegetables, meat and shrimps. Siopao is ground rice in patties steamed with meat inside; lumpia has finely chopped meat and vegetables wrapped in special wrappers and eaten with sauce; lugaw is rice cooked with chicken meat and plenty of broth.

The Chinese mind, a blend of philosophy and pragmatism, has been transplanted into the Filipino psyche. Patience and perseverance, hardiness and foresight, frugality and thrift have been infused into the Filipino character by the Chinese. The Chinese ideal of filial piety, the emphasis on man as a social being and "sageliness within and kingliness without" ideal have been carried over into Filipino life. Thus for a Filipino, relations between parents and children and lateral relatives is a matter of ethics and honor. Getting along with one's neighbors is a fundamental prerequisite to prosperity, happiness and human existence. Sageliness or self-improvement by cultivation of virtue and personal worth and wisdom is evident in the Filipino national passion for education. Elaborate dress, pride of place, ritual and etiquette, propriety and wealth and class distinctions are signs of Kingliness.

One of the prime values for the Filipino-Chinese is filial piety. The almost blind obedience to parents seems to Westerners a thing of utter dependence on elders. But the Filipino-Chinese think that elders certainly have more experience in living and they have the prerogative to make decisions for their sons and daughters. Thus the Filipino-Chinese are erroneously called "yellow-race" which connotes cowardice. Westerners call the Chinese "yellow" because when a Chinese wanted to intervene or fight for revenge, the elders told him not to.

The Indian influence in the Filipinos is manifested in the

Filipino traditions, customs, modes of dressing, architectural art, brass and copperware. Much of the ancient Filipino religious beliefs are features of the Bhraman religion of India. Folk beliefs such as when a person dreams his teeth have fallen out, one of his friends or relatives will die is Indian; or that going to bed before recently washed hair has completely dried will lead to insanity or that a thorn in one's throat can be cured by a cat's paw. Although the Filipinos have had some Indian influence, they refuse to be called "Indio" (Indian). This appelation was used by the Spaniards to call the natives of the Philippines with a pejorative sense, meaning "uncivilized or uncultured."

The Spanish Strain in the Filipino

Spain brought to the Filipinos the Christian religion and the western social organization. It gave the Filipinos the Spanish law, the Spanish language, and a certain Spanishness in the national character. The names of Filipinos are Spanish. The Filipino dialects have borrowed and absorbed thousands of Spanish words. The family rituals of Sunday worship and public holidays are Spanish. Mourning, and courting customs are mainly Spanish. The religion of 80 percent of Filipinos is Spanish Catholicism, although it is based upon a folk Christianity that still sets great store of pre-Spanish superstitions and pagan beliefs.

Many of the social standards of Filipino life are Spanish in origin. The combination of generosity and arrogance in the Filipino is Spanish. The emphasis on appearance, reputation, privilege and status, and *delicadeza* among Filipinos are all Spanish.

The American in the Filipino

The English language, mass education, public health and a system of roads are the American contributions to Filipino life. America gave Filipinos the modern mechanics and the techniques of Westernized democracy. America taught the Filipinos to ask two questions: "Does it work" and, "What has he done?" America introduced to the Filipinos the Protestant ethic of rationality, of questioning, of independent thinking, and of direct communication.

13

The Filipino was exposed to everything American due to stateside movies, books, television, magazines, etc. Thus the Filipino has acquired a state-side mentality.

Regional Difference among Filipinos

There are regional differences among Filipinos as they are influenced by different economic conditions and geographical locations. The Filipino is known to be a spendthrift if he comes from the Tagalog region, the Visayas or Pampanga, but an icorrigible tightwad if he comes from the Northern provinces. Filipinos from the sugar area enjoy better credit facilities and are loose with their money, whereas the Ilocanos are generally industrious and thrifty with their hard earned money. The Visayan Filipinos live in rich lands, with very fertile soil that does not require much tilling to make it productive. The Filipinos from Visayas, therefore, do not have to work too hard to enjoy a bountiful harvest. This tends to make them a little lazy, a little easy going, since they have more leisure time. Most Ilocanos from north Ilocandia live in places where the soil is rough, barren and rocky. It needs backbreaking work to get it to produce. Hence, for survival the Filipino Ilocanos have to work long, hard hours. This makes them industrious and because of unreliable harvests, they become ultra thrifty with their earnings.

The Filipino can be illiterate, if he comes from a miserable rural family beyond the pale of public schools; but he can also be a savant if he comes from a middle class family close to the arteries of education. He can be an impoverished farmer cooped up with his family in a tiny nipa hut in the barrio, or a wealthy and powerful aristocrat living in a magnificent mansion at Forbes Park.

There are 111 linguistic, cultural and racial groups in the Philippines. The major linguistic groups are the following: Tagalog, Cebuano, Ilocano, Hiligaynon, Bicol, Waray, Pampango, Pangasinan and Maranao. While the Philippines has a national language called Pilipino, English remains the language of instruction in the secondary and tertiary schools and is almost universally understood. The Philippines is the third largest English-speaking nation in the world. Spanish, Arabic, and Chinese are spoken by a small minority.

14

Religions in the Philippines

Historically, the Filipinos have embraced two of the great religions of the world—Islam and Christianity. Islam was introduced during the 14th century, shortly after the expansion of Arab commercial ventures in Southeast Asia. By the 16th century it was extending its influence northward when the Spaniards came to curb its spread. Today, it is limited mainly to the southern region of the country. Scholars have pointed out that, as it exists today, Islam has undergone tremendous cultural accommodation. This means that its official doctrine has been reinterpreted in terms of local ways of thinking, doing, and believing. Westerners who intend to go to the southern region of the Philippines must have in mind that they are in the Muslim part of the country. Filipino Muslims do not wish to be called "moors" or "moros" as the Spanish colonizers called them before. The word "Moro" carries with it a pejorative meaning.

Catholic Christianity

Christianity was introduced as early as the 16th century with the coming of Ferdinand Magellan in 1521. However, it did not become firmly established until the 17th century when the Spaniards decided to make the Philippines one of their colonies. The doctrinal teachings were based on Roman Catholicism. For several centuries, the Philippines has remained predominantly a Catholic country.

Other Religions

Protestantism was introduced to the country in 1899 when the first Presbyterian and Methodist missionaries arrived with the American soldiers during the Spanish-American War. Following closely were the Baptists (1900), the Episcopalians, the Disciples of Christ, the Evangelical United Brethren (1901) and the Congregationalists who came in 1902. Since then, many other Protestant denominations have come.

Locally, two Filipino independent churches were organized at the turn of the 20th century and are prominent today. These are the Aglipay (Philippine Independent Church) and the Iglesia Ni Cristo (Church of Christ) founded in 1902 and 1914, respectively. Recently, the Aglipayans signed a covenant with the Anglican Church. The Iglesia Ni Cristo, on the other hand, has expanded its membership considerably. In fact, the Iglesia Ni Kristo Church, with its unique towering architecture, is a prodigious sight in almost all important towns, provincial capitals and major cities of the country.

Split-Level Christianity

Among some Filipino Catholics there exists the phenomenon called *split-level Christianity*. This consists of the co-existence within the same person of two or more thought and behavior systems which are inconsistent with each other. This split-leveling involves the absence of a sense of guilt, or the presence of only a very minimal amount. One who practices a split-level religiosity is convinced that two objectively inconsistent thought-and-behavior systems really fit each other. This inconsistency is either not perceived at all, or is pushed into the rear portions of consciousness. Hence the feeling of inconsistency and hypocrisy does not arise. This inconsistency remains in the unconsciousness or in the semi-consciousness until an authority figure discovers the existence of the split. Split-leveling is the practical way one learns to handle the opposing pressures of two distinct groups holding different value systems. Desirous to please two groups possessing opposing value systems, one solves the dilemma of both pressures by keeping them apart and by simply ignoring the inconsistencies. Some illustrations of such split-leveling are the following:

A. A Filipino is very religious but at the same time very superstitious. Examples of Filipino superstitions are the following:[4]

Superstitions and Beliefs Related to Death:

1. If a black butterfly lingers around a person, it means that one of his relatives has just died.
2. No one should go out before the utensils used in eating have been washed and put away, otherwise a member of the family will die.

16

3. One must not organize teams of 3 or 13, otherwise one member will die.

4. Eating sour fruits at night will cause the early death of one's parents.

5. At a funeral, not all members of the family should be allowed to look at the face of the dead person. If they do, he will visit them and all of them will die.

6. If a sick person on his way to the hospital meets a black cat, he will die.

7. If someone smells the odor of a candle when there is no candle burning, one of his relatives will die.

8. If one dreams that one of his teeth is being uprooted or pulled out, a member of his family will die.

9. If a person eats "malunggay" (leaves of a Philippine tree used as a vegetable) when one member of his family has just died, all the other members of the family will die.

10. During a wedding the one whose candle goes out first will be the first of the couple to die.

11. If one cuts his fingernails at night, a member of the family will die.

12. When a group of three have their picture taken, the one in the middle will die first.

13. If a cock crows in the afternoon, it means somebody will die.

14. If an owl is seen near the house of a sick person, that sick person is sure to die.

15. Pregnant women should not have their picture taken; otherwise, their babies will die.

16. While the mother is giving birth, every hole in the house should be covered, otherwise an evil spirit might come in and kill the baby.

17. When a pregnant woman wears a black dress, her baby will die.

18. If a person's shadow appears to be without a head, that person will soon die.

19. Cleaning the backyard when the sun has already set and it is already dark causes death.

20. If two people from the same family get married within a year, one will die.

21. If you place a dead person with his feet pointing toward the rising sun, a relative will die.

On Bad Luck or Misfortune

1. The bride should not try on her wedding dress before the wedding ceremony; otherwise, the wedding will not take place.
2. If one meets a black cat while crossing the road, a misfortune will occur.
3. If during the time a house is being built the carpenter meets with an accident, the owner of the house will have misfortune in life.
4. A girl who sings before a stove while she cooks will be married to an old widower.
5. If a pregnant woman cuts her hair, she will give birth to a hairless child.
6. One should not decorate a dress with pearls because it means she will shed tears.
7. One should not sit on his books because it will make him dull.
8. A boy who sleeps on a table will someday marry a widow.
9. When an adolescent plays, it will rain.
10. A couple will not be happy in their marriage if loud thunder occurs during their wedding.
11. One should not pay or give money through the window because it will make him poor.
12. If one brings salt near an orange tree, the tree will start to bear sour fruit.
13. When a duck flies it is a sign of bad luck.
14. One should not comb his hair in front of the body of a dead person or else all his hair will fall off.
15. When a cat washes himself, a storm is coming.
16. One does not eat in front of a stove for this causes wealth to go away.
17. A pregnant woman should not eat twin bananas for it causes twin births.
18. If one throws a stone in the dark at night, he will harm someone.
19. If a pregnant woman eats a red star apple, she will give birth to a child who will look like a star apple.
20. One should not stand in front of a burned house. It will cause his own house to be burned.

21. If one opens an umbrella inside the house, a lizard from the ceiling will fall.
22. When many butterflies are flying, it means rain will come.
23. If one sees a snake while he is on his way to the cockpit, it means bad luck.
24. If one puts a stick into the mouth of a glass she will see the face of her future husband.
25. Sweeping the floor at night causes one to lose all his wealth.
26. If one breaks a glass, a plate or a cup during a banquet, something bad will happen.
27. After hearing mass, one must not take a bath because the holy water will be removed from his body.
28. Debts should not be paid at night. It brings bad luck.
29. Pregnant women should not sit on the stairs because that might make their deliveries difficult.
30. When the frogs cry, it will rain.
31. A pregnant woman who goes to the river will give birth to a dead baby.
32. One will have bad luck if he breaks a mirror.
33. If one points his finger at a rainbow, his finger will be cut off.
34. When the ants start to climb up the house, it will rain.
35. Women who have moles under the eyes, where the tears fall, will be widowed.
36. The woman who eats crabs during pregnancy will have a baby with six fingers or with other physical deformities.
37. If one reconstructs his house, he should not cut the posts because that might cause him to lose his wealth.
38. The family that lives in a house in which the stairs face the sun will have bad luck.
39. If one removes the plates while an unmarried woman is still eating, that woman will stay single all her life.
40. Playing at night brings bad luck.
41. During menstruation a woman should not touch or pinch plants, otherwise, the plants will die.
42. During the Holy Week, people should not go out or travel in order to avoid accidents.
43. Old clothes given to other people will only bring them bad luck.
44. Whistling in the evening is bad.

45. Drying clothes, especially underwear, at night causes pregnancy.
46. If a single lady dreams of a wedding, she will become an old maid.
47. If one has to pass between two houses close to each other, he should murmur some words (such as *"makikiraan po"* may I pass).
48. If one breaks something he is holding in his hand, it means bad luck.
49. If one kills a cat, he will suffer persecution for seven years.
50. If a picture falls from a wall, it means bad luck.
51. If a hen cackles under the house at night, it means a girl in the family will give birth to an illegitimate child.
52. A pregnant woman should not eat raw rice during pregnancy, otherwise, she will have a toothless baby.
53. If a person leaves the house while others are eating, they should turn their plates around so that he will not meet with an accident.
54. If one receives a present that is pointed (like a knife or a letter opener) he should give the giver a rounded object (like a five or ten centavo piece).
55. When one goes to his wedding, he should not ride in a bus to avoid bad luck.
56. One should cover the mirror when there is lightning to avoid misfortune.
57. If one winnows the rice in the doorway, he will have a small harvest the next year.
58. Changing clothes twice before going to church means something bad will happen on the way.
59. Never tell about a dream before breakfast because this will cause misfortune.
60. If one happens to break the eggs of a lizard, he will also break something in the home.
61. If a woman in the family way watches a burial, she will have a difficult delivery.
62. One who tells jokes about saints will be punished by having his fists closed forever.
63. Throwing rice or salt on the floor makes one as poor as a rat.
64. If one takes an unbaptized baby out of the house, he will meet with an accident.

For Good Luck

1. Throwing rice at newlyweds will bring prosperity throughout their life and they will have good children.
2. If one catches the bride's bouquet after a wedding ceremony, she will also get married soon.
3. One should open his window early in the morning so that grace will come in.
4. A baby born with a big birthmark on its body will be lucky.
5. If one's palm becomes itchy, she will receive some money.
6. When one sees a snake crossing the street, he will have good luck.
7. The placenta should be buried so that the baby will not be a problem child.
8. A person with big ears will have a long life.
9. A baby born with an extra finger is lucky.
10. If a baby cries during his baptism ceremony, it will have a long life.
11. Wishing on the first star that one sees in the evening will make that wish come true.
12. Parents with a child who is a deaf mute are lucky.

On Illnesses

1. Sleeping with wet hair causes blindness.
2. A person will get sick if he takes a bath on Friday.
3. If one removes ear wax at night, he will become deaf the following week.
4. A person who cuts his fingernails at night will become sick.
5. A person who cuts his fingernails on Friday will have a serious illness.
6. Before throwing hot water on the ground, give a warning to the elves, otherwise you will become sick.
7. Playing with one's shadow will make one crazy.
8. Warts are caused by the urine of frogs.
9. Bathing during menstruation period causes insanity.
10. Eating sour food during menstruation causes stomach trouble.
11. Drinking dog's blood is a cure for tuberculosis.
12. Eating *bugok* eggs (partially incubated eggs without the embryo) will make a person dull.

On the Coming of Visitors

1. If a fork drops to the floor accidentally, a male visitor is coming; if a spoon, a female visitor will come.
2. When a cat sitting by the door cleans its paws or rubs its face, a visitor is coming.
3. When a house lizard makes a noise, a visitor will come.
4. When someone sings in front of a fire while cooking, a visitor is coming soon.

On Ghosts, Spirits and Witches

1. If one passes through the window instead of the door, a ghost will come.
2. When two dogs bark at night there is a ghost.
3. Before six o'clock at night, children should be in the house or else they may bump into a person without a head.
4. When one passes by an anthill, one should ask to be excused, otherwise, a spirit will play tricks on that person.
5. A person who always uses a bandage on Fridays is a witch.

Break Up of Relationships

1. No marriage should take place except during the period of the full moon. It is the belief that good fortune comes only during that period.
2. Giving religious articles to one's sweetheart will cause breaking up of the relationship.
3. If a person gives another a pair of shoes as a gift, they will become enemies.

On War, Pestilence and Calamity

1. Appearance of a comet foretells war, pestilence and calamity.
2. When a star gets near the moon, it is an omen of war.

Other Superstitions and Beliefs

1. If a person bites his tongue, it means somebody is thinking of him.
2. A girl with white spots on her fingernails is inconstant in love.

3. It is bad to sweep the floor at six o'clock in the evening for it means driving away good fortune and graces.

4. It is bad to sweep the floor when there are people playing cards or gambling because luck is being swept away.

5. One should not open an umbrella while inside a house; a centipede is likely to fall from the ceiling and he will be bitten by it.

6. If a pregnant woman sews her dress while wearing it, her baby will be born without a hole in the rectum.

7. If a pregnant woman sits on the stairs, she will have a difficult time in delivering her baby.

8. If a pregnant woman wears a necklace or a choker, the umbilical cord of her baby will also be wound around its neck endangering its life.

9. If the direction of the wooden slats of a floor are not parallel to the stairs, good fortune will not come to the dwellers of the house.

10. If sweethearts give each other gifts like shoes or slippers, their relationship will not last long.

11. If a boy gives his sweetheart a necklace as a gift and the necklace is broken, it means that they are not meant for each other.

12. If the coffin of a dead person bumps against something during the funeral, someone will soon die.

13. If the coffin of a dead person is too big for his size, someone will also die soon.

14. In bringing the coffin down the house, the head should be the first so that the dead will have an easy journey to his destiny.

15. The dead in the coffin should face the rising sun upon interment so that his soul will not suffer very much.

16. If two sisters or two brothers get married within the same year, one will have a prosperous married life; the other, a sorrowful life.

17. If a couple receives a urinal as a wedding gift they will have luck, prosperity and riches.

18. If a couple receives a crucifix as a wedding gift, they will have a peaceful relationship.

19. In a church wedding ceremony, the first of the couple to reach the altar and to go out of the church will be the dominant one.

20. If the veil sponsor in the wedding ceremony is still single, she is doomed to be an old maid.

21. He whose candle is put off during the wedding ceremony will die first.

22. If a pregnant woman looks beautiful and kind, she will have a baby girl; if she looks ugly and cruel, she will have a baby boy.

23. A pregnant woman who gives birth to a baby boy will have a painful delivery; one who has a girl will have an easy delivery.

24. If one combs his hair at night, his parents will die.

25. If one puts his used plates over those of others while some are still eating, the last one to leave the table will have many problems.

26. If one gives a wallet or a bag as a gift, he must put some money in it or else such wallet or bag will bring bad luck.

27. Counting money on the midnights of December 24 up to January 1 of the New Year will bring a person endless wealth during the whole year.

28. One must pay all his debts before January 1st of the New Year or else he will always be in debt the whole year.

29. Rice bags and salt containers in the home must always be full to maintain a bountiful life.

30. On Good Fridays one must not do hard work, take a bath, eat meat or make any noise because "God is dead."

31. On Easter Sunday, all children must jump high upon hearing the sound of the church Easter bells so that they will grow taller.

32. There must be a feast or banquet on Easter Sunday to celebrate the new life of Jesus Christ.

33. When a person receives as a gift a statue of Buddha with children around him, the receiver will be lucky with his children.

34. When a person receives as a gift a statue of Buddha without children around him, the receiver's business will fail.

35. If one receives a jade stone or his own birth stone as a gift, he will be lucky in life.

36. If one receives a diamond as a gift, he will be lucky in business.

37. Putting a statue of Sto. Niño (The Holy Child) in one's store or business place brings good luck.

38. One must make the sign of the cross before he leaves his house or before taking a long journey so that he will arrive safely at his destination.
39. If one breaks a mirror, he will have seven years of bad luck.
40. Upon transfering to a new house, the occupants must bring rice and salt first so that they will have a prosperous life in that house.
41. If a relative dies, the children related to the dead must be lifted across the coffin before it is put into the grave so that the soul of the dead will not visit them.
42. During interment of the dead, the children should wear red clothes so that the soul of the dead will not bother them.
43. The people in the first house to which a newly-baptized child is brought should voluntarily give some money so that a good and prosperous life will come to the child.
44. Eating peanuts makes a person intelligent.
45. If parents want their child to be a good orator or speaker when he grows, they must feed him with the cooked female organ of a pig.
46. If the umbilical cord of a baby is inserted in the staircase of the house, its grasp will be strong.
47. If red ants are abundant in a certain part of a house, good fortune will come to the occupants of the house.
48. If one's left palm is itchy, money is coming to him; if his right palm is itchy, money will be spent by him.
49. If a black butterfly enters the house, someone in the family will die.
50. If a baby is born with a mole on his forehead, he will grow up an intelligent man.
51. If a baby is born with a mole on his shoulder, he will have a lot of hardships and sorrow in life.
52. If a baby is born with a mole on his foot, he will travel a lot.
53. If a baby is born with a mole near his eye, he will be easily widowed, and for several times.
54. When the temporary tooth of a child is extracted, that tooth should be thrown out with a request that the rats should give him another new and fine tooth.
55. Broken mirrors or glasses in the house should be removed; otherwise, good luck will not come to that house.
56. A man with natural curly hair is temperamental and moody.

57. A man with a hairline that is elongated at the back is stingy.
58. A man with a deep nape is stingy.
59. A woman with a mole at the nape will have many suitors.
60. A child with two cowlicks on his head is a hard-headed but lucky child.
61. There should be "pansit" or noodles in a birth celebration so that the celebrant will have a long life.
62. If there is a pregnant woman in a house, garlic, vinegar and a bolo should be placed on the window so that vampires will not eat the fetus.
63. A woman who has just delivered a baby should take hot soup after her first bath so that she will regain her youthful skin.
64. If one wants to be remembered by a friend, she should put that friend's picture under her own pillow when she sleeps at night.
65. Upon entering a town church for the first time, one should make a wish so that good luck will come to him.
66. In constructing a house, silver coins or cash money are put within the principal posts so that prosperity will come to the dwellers of that house.
67. If one gets lost on his way to a certain place, he should invert his shirt and he will find his way.
68. A woman with thick and rounded heels is by nature lazy.
69. A person with a flat foot is by nature a slow-foot.
70. A person with a wide forehead is intelligent.
71. A person with a narrow forehead is dull.
72. A person with a mole on the lips is talkative.
73. A person with a mole between the two eyes is lucky in business.
74. A person with a wide shoulder is lazy.
75. One must not spend money on a Monday because money will be going out of his pocket the whole week.
76. A businessman must make sure that his first customer on Mondays buys from him, otherwise business the whole week will not be good.
77. A sponsor in a house blessing must toss coins as he holds a lighted candle inside the house so that prosperity and good luck will come to the dwellers.

78. Lending or giving out rice from your house at night brings bad luck.
79. The main door of the house should face the rising sun so that good luck and abundance will come inside the house.
80. Using broken plates inside the house brings bad luck.
81. Flowerpots should not be placed one over the other because there will be misfortune for the family year after year.
82. When there is hard rain and strong lightning, one should spray vinegar all over the house and cover all the mirrors so that the lightning will not strike the house.
83. A baby's eyelashes should be cut short within its first three months so that they will grow long and curly.
84. A newly-born baby should be tossed up into the air after its first bath so that it will not grow up a frightful person.
85. Changing the name of a baby who is criticaly ill may save his life.
86. Cutting one's fingernails on days when the Sorrowful Mysteries is prayed brings bad luck.
87. When a person changes his place from one to another while eating, he will be unfaithful to his life partner.
88. Sweeping the floor when there is a wake for the dead in that house is never done because someone else in the family will also die.
89. Helping a baby to turn on its stomach for the first time is not good for it will grow up a very dependent person.
90. One must avoid giving handkerchiefs as gifts because the recipient of the handkerchiefs is likely to cause grief to the giver.
91. Sweethearts should not be baptismal sponsors of the same child; otherwise, their relationship will not end up in marriage.
92. A pregnant woman should not have her picture taken because her baby will be born abnormal.
93. A pregnant woman should not act as a baptismal sponsor because her baby might die.
94. The first time a baby lies face down, he should be placed sitting on a basin so that he will be wealthy when he grows up.
95. A hungry person must not greet a child; otherwise, the child will grow thin from a bad stomach ache.
96. During the first three months of a woman's pregnancy, she

should not be fond of babies or else she will vomit and become uncomfortable.

97. During the period of intense craving felt by a conceiving woman, she should not take notice of fruit-bearing trees for the trees might die.

98. A woman who sings while cooking will not be able to marry throughout her life.

99. A younger child in the family should not get married ahead of the older one because misfortune will befall him; the older one may not get married anymore.

100. Bad luck will come to the dwellers of a house whose last step of the stairs faces the main exit of the house.

101. Houses on dead end street should not have gates directly facing the street; otherwise, an occupant of the house will die from an accident.

102. If tears are shed on the coffin of the dead, the soul of the dead person will never have peace.

103. When there are cats fighting in the neighborhood, children of one family will soon also be fighting one another.

104. When one goes to borrow money from a friend and on the way a cat crosses his path, she should not go on with his intention because the cat is an indication that his friend will not lend him money.

105. Talking when eating something is an act of rejecting God's grace.

106. Visitors should be asked to enter the house at once and not stop at the door or else the pregnant woman in the house will have some suffering.

107. The new-born should be given *ampalaya* (bitter melon) juice before the first breast feeding to improve the baby's appetite and prevent his becoming choosey or finicky about food when he grows up.

108. The child's bath should be withheld on Fridays to prevent his developing serious illness.

109. The baby's first nail trimmings should be buried under the stairway to prevent falls.

110. The placenta should be buried near the kitchen to keep both mother and baby healthy.

111. The cord stump should be carefully watched and kept immediately if it falls off, for if a mouse gets hold of it the baby would be sickly.

wind passes by, he will develop a squint.
31. An evil spirit usually goes with the fragrance of flowers at night. Anyone who smells it would also suck in the evil spirit who will eat the bridge of the nose until it crumbles down.
32. Every temporary tooth of a child that falls off should be buried in the moist earth under the *batalan* (an open bathroom next to the kitchen of a Filipino nipa house) so that it may be replaced by a permanent tooth that is resistant to decay.
33. Any person delivered breech or buttocks or feet first has the special power to remove fish spines in the throat of others either by simply applying his hands or handkerchief on the neck or by rubbing his saliva over it.
34. A sacrifice should be offered in newly opened forest areas to _____ irits that are present in those places.

_____ ss, vernacularly called *binat, begnat,* or _____ g certain kinds of food or by cutting _____ ss. This relapse is best treated by _____ noke produced by burning the _____ ir.

_____ ers around, for a time at _____ nt. To keep this soul _____ ves, and friends, _____ na should be

_____ or any-

112. To ensure a bright future for the child, the mother places coins, papers, pencils or diamond rings in the basin used for his first bath.
113. Eczematous children are dressed in black clothes to make the course of the disease shorter.
114. Skin eruptions are treated with saliva and chewed *buyo* leaves applied on the skin.
115. A house in which a member of the family dies is burned or abandoned to prevent illness and death of the other members of the family.
116. Seven (7) is a lucky number and all other odd numbers are lucky.
117. The premature delivery of a baby is an evidence of "sin."

B. Some Filipino Christians believe in the existence and power of *anitos* (minor deities which are revered and esteemed as intermediaries to God); they believe in the power of quacks and faith-healers to cure certain ailments that physicians could not; they believe in the power of witches to inflict illness on any individual who has incurred their displeasure. Many Filipino Christians still cling to ancient beliefs and practices. Superstition is a fixed irrational idea; a notion maintained in spite of evidence to the contrary. A person may be said to be superstitious if he believes in, is addicted to, or is swayed by ideas or notions contrary to reason or scientific knowledge.

Common among Filipinos is the belief that sickness is the work of some evil spirits. Examples of such beliefs are the following:[5]

1. When a child has epileptic fits or when a pregnant woman has convulsive seizures, an evil spirit is supposed to have entered the body of the child or of the woman.
2. When some painful and red spots appear suddenly on the body of a person who came from the field or from a thicket, an invisible hand is suspected to have mischievously touched the person.
3. When a man has a stroke of paralysis, an evil wind is believed to have hit him.
4. When a tumor grows in a part of the body, a displeased witch or a person who has contact with an evil spirit is

thought to have planted it.

5. When a member of the family has persistent fever, the spirit of a deceased relative is presumed to remind the family of an unfulfilled obligation to the departed soul.

6. To scare the spirits away and to cure those afflicted by the evil spirits, the curative practices are: to flog the patient, put signs of the cross on his forehead or at every post of his house, and make all kinds of noises; sacrifice some live animals or offer some food, buyo and oil to appease the offended spirit; and wear amulets (*anting-anting*) to neutralize the machinations of the devil.

7. When a sick person is seriously ill or is pronounced by reputable physicians as hopeless or incurable, he and his family have that instinctive urge to resort to the cure of the magicians, wizards, sorcerers, voodoos, mystics, conjurers, *manghihilot* (sprain curer), *herbolarios*, or faith-healer, be it of dubious value. Remorse comes if they do not resort to such a practice because as a result of breaking away from old beliefs and practices, someone in the family might keep saying ever afterward, "If only we had done this, the patient might have pulled through."

8. After biting a person, the dog is killed to protect its victim from contracting rabies.

9. The heat or moisture of the earth neutralizes the snake venom in a snakebite.

10. Many people leave their skin diseases untreated because of the belief that these ailments serve as outlets for noxious substances produced in the body.

11. A red patch of skin is the result of the mischivous "touch" of an invisible hand of an anito.

12. No two pregnant women should live under a common roof lest one meet with a tragic accident.

13. Delivering twins is a result of eating twin bananas or looking at twin objects.

14. A child in the womb might be marked in some obscure way by what the mother has thought, felt, or seen during pregnancy. Thus, a pregnant woman should refrain from seeing horror movies and looking at grotesque pictures in comic magazines and advertising billboards.

15. All the wishes of the pregnant woman should be satisfied lest miscarriage take place. A husband should inquire most

solicitously about all that his pregnant wife to possess.

16. A pregnant woman should not go out at nigh hangs her hair loose. A vampire (*aswang*) might t suck her blood or that of her fetus.

17. Tying the umbilical cord of a baby girl with a st hanging it in the front part of the house will give th girl many suitors when she grows up.

18. Air should not be allowed to seep through the skin or ge organ of a woman who has just delivered a baby. Otherwi the woman and the baby will have frequent attacks of col or the mother will be insane.

19. Certain varieties of fruits and vegetables like eggplants, squash, *gabi* and arrowroots should be excluded from the diet of a woman who has just given birth colic in the newly-born baby or genital organs of the mother.

20. A woman who has just deli unpolished rice mixed wit

21. A pregnant woman sh cause swelling of her

22. The baby's umbi edge of a baby su would

23. Wh

1. The lucky dates of the twelve months of the year are the following:[6]

January 1, 3, 4, 5, 28, 29
February 2, 4, 5, 17, 26, 27, 28
March 2, 3, 8, 9, 10
April 2, 6, 25, 26, 27
May 1, 2, 3, 4, 12, 13, 18, 20
June 3, 5, 16, 19, 24, 30
July 4, 12, 15, 19, 26
August 6, 9, 14, 19, 26, 31
September 3, 12, 20, 21, 29
October 7, 12, 17, 24, 29, 30
November 1, 2, 11, 18, 23, 28
December 5, 8, 16, 20, 24, 25

2. The unlucky three 18ths of the three months are:

March 18
September 18
August 18

3. The lucky dates for planting are the following:

In January: 3, 5, 8, 9, 10, 18, 21, 28, 29, 30, 31
In February: 2, 4, 5, 6, 12, 13, 17, 18, 24, 26
In March: 3, 8, 9, 10, 14, 16, 25, 26, 28, 29
In April: 1, 4, 11, 12, 14, 21, 22, 26, 27
In May: 1, 3, 5, 8, 9, 10, 12, 18, 19, 29, 30, 31
In June: 7, 8, 10, 16, 19, 22, 24, 25, 26, 27
In July: 3, 4, 5, 6, 7, 14, 23, 24, 25, 29, 30, 31
In August: 1, 3, 4, 5, 11, 12, 21, 22, 26, 27, 28
In September: 1, 3, 8, 9, 10, 19, 20, 28, 29, 30
In October: 3, 7, 10, 12, 16, 17, 21, 22, 26, 27
In November: 3, 4, 5, 10, 13, 14, 19, 20, 24, 27, 30
In December: 1, 2, 9, 10, 11, 12, 24, 25, 27, 29, 31

4. The four unlucky Mondays of the months are:

a) Monday of April, when God condemned the towns of Beram, Lipandas, Madama, Sodom and Gomorrah
b) Monday of August,, when Eve gave birth to Cain
c) Monday of September, when Judas Escariot was born
d) Monday of January, when Cain killed Abel

D. *Filipino Norm of Morality*. Sometimes there is a conflict between what some Filipino Christians *say* as Christians and what they *do*. One norm of morality in the Philippines is based on "group-centeredness" or "group-thinking."7 One's in-group determines for the individual what is right or wrong. "What other people will say" usually determines Filipino moral behavior. His conscience is influenced from the outside—"What his family, his relatives and friends, or his peer group (*barkada*) think or say" is what counts.

E. *Folk Catholicism*. The early Filipinos believed in *Batula*, the supreme god, who was so aloof and distant that to seek favors from Batula they had to pray to the lesser spirits or anitos who were the guardian gods in whose honor pagan rituals or rice festivals were held. With the coming of Christianity, the native Filipinos substituted the Christian God for Batula, the town patronal saints for the anitos, and the town and barrio fiestas for the pagan rice festivals. The parish priest took the place of the *baylan*.

F. *Fiestas*. Fiestas may be held any time of the year but the biggest if not the best of them takes place in May, the month between the harvest and the planting, when farmers, fishermen and factory workers take time out for a well-earned rest and a bit of merrymaking.

On May 15, farming communities in the country, particularly those in Southern Luzon, honor San Isidro Labrador, the patron saint of farmers, with exuberant displays of the fruit of the land. The displays are always extravagant and unrestrained. If the harvests were abundant, to do less would be considered ungrateful. And if the harvests were lean, the lavish display reminds the patron saint to do better by the farmers the next year.

Nowhere else in the world, perhaps, is as much tribute and homage given to the food god than in the coconut-producing towns of Quezon province. For weeks before the 15th of May regular work stops and all the towns folk busy themselves in preparing buntings and delicacies that will hang from windows and bamboo poles around the town. The display is called *pahi-yas* or "decor" which implies that the harvest has been abundant;

that ripe palay stalks, big bunches of bananas, long bean pods, bright red tomatoes, everything grown and fruited of the land is so plentiful that they can be used for decoration. The celebration shows the Filipinos' love for ritual and spectacle. In keeping with the tradition of thanksgiving for a good harvest, no visitor is allowed to go home empty-handed. Food is almost literally pushed down one's throat; it is an insult to decline an invitation to eat. Houses are opened up even to total strangers; and the belief is that no one has really been proven a loser by such a reckless gesture of hospitality.

The greatest number of fiestas is celebrated in honor of Mary, Queen of May. Some are small, private affairs like the daily offerings of flowers carried by little girls in the rituals called *Flores de Mayo* (the Flowers of May). Some are community-wide rituals, like the evening candlelight processions called *Santa Cruz de Mayo*, which commemorate Saint Helena's finding of the Cross on which Christ was crucified. This celebration often combines a religious event with a beauty contest, since only the town's most beautiful young woman is deemed worthy to portray St. Helena and only its handsomest young man, her son, the Emperor Constantine.

The Obando Festival is held on May 17, 18 and 19 in Obando, a rustic country town in Bulacan province, about an hour's drive from Manila. It is an event in which childless elderly women and young wives implore the help of Mary, Saint Clare and Saint Pascual, the town's patrons, that they might conceive and bear children. They all sing and dance to the melody of a tune.

Another interesting fiesta is that which takes place every May in the hill town of Pakil, Laguna. Before a very old picture of the Blessed Mother, devotees sing, hop, skip and leap. The procession through the streets of Pakil often gets so giddy and frisky that it ends with a happy leap into the town's public swimming pool.

For the Filipino, the fiesta is the ultimate gesture of respect and esteem. He who does not celebrate it is taken to be rude, for the fiesta is a time for showing appreciation to the saints for favors received, for favors done. It is a time for establishing social positions, or for redefining it if necessary. It is a time for paying back debts, not the outright payables, but debts of gratitude and honor.

G. *Novenas.* In a Catholic community where the fiesta celebrates the day named after the town patron, the celebration necessarily centers on the church. Novenas—nine days of prayer—anticipate the feast. On the day itself, bells peal to announce the liturgical services; bands of musicians roam the town rousing the people and reminding them of the evening procession in honor of the patron. At nearly every fiesta a pair of prominent citizens are chosen to manage the celebration. Many times they volunteer to spend their own money, for this is considered a form of gratitude for favors received in the past.

As the novena progresses, the secular features of the fiesta also take shape. These are the fairs and the carnival managed by modern-day gypsies who move from town to town, carrying in cargo trucks chipped game stalls, ferris wheels and wheel-o-whirls, and wire-coiled motors.

Some Filipino Catholics make novenas to obtain favors from God. They tend to treat God as a *compadre* from whom can be obtained favors or as a policeman whom he can bribe by means of a novena.

H. *Anthropomorphic Conception of God.* Many Filipinos treat God as an equal on a person to person basis by means of "smooth interpersonal relations." When they feel that they have done something for God, they expect Him to reciprocate. If ill fortune befalls them, they consider it a punishment from God and the thing to do then is to talk it over with God personally.

Similarly, children are taught that they must never disobey their parents, show disrespect for elders, waste food, or do what is forbidden, or else the *gaba* (curse) will fall upon them. Everything is a "spilling over" of God. The rain is the "tear of God," the colors of Nature as the "Smiles of God," the typhoons and earthquakes are the "wrath of God," etc.

The Filipino sees, hears, feels, touches and smells God in every quiver of a leaf, in every drop of rain, in every passing breeze. That is why planting and harvesting and fishing in the Philippines are intimately tied up with worship and cult. There is a *diwata* (fairy) or anito or *patron* for every place and event. The Filipino articulates this presence of God through symbols. He is fond of rituals and external manifestations of piety. Candles, incense, processions, statues, medals, ritual dancing,

36

ritual devotion to the invisible dead, etc. are the more common visible articulations of the Filipino's contemplative sense of the invisible. A Westerner who does not understand all these things may ridicule all these as primitive and superstitious but the Filipino has all these as his own indigenous spirituality and theology. This the Westerner may never understand but must respect.

I. *The Compadre System.* Ritual kinship was introduced as part of the Christian culture to ensure a godchild's education in the faith. This kinship is acquired immediately during the Christian's performance of the sacraments of baptism and confirmation. After such ceremonies, the godparents immediately become the "compadre" of the child's parents. The "compadre system" not only establishes itself between godparents and parents but also among godparents in case of multiple godparents.

In the official Catholic laws, no statement is mentioned about the spiritual relationship between witnesses and the bridal pair, but the Filipino ingenuity has transformed these sacraments as another source of the "compadre system." The bridal pairs become the "godchildren" and the godparents and parents have established the "compadre system" among themselves.

The official Catholic teachings demand that the godparents to be chosen for a child to be baptized should first and foremost be a Catholic. However, since for some Filipino Christians the usage of the sacraments to create a compadre system has become exploitative, anyone who has power or wealth, whether Catholic or not, is asked to be the godparent in the baptism of a child. Thus, a non-Catholic vice-president for administration in a company may be asked many times by his Catholic subordinates to become the godfather of their children to ensure their employment or promotion. Since in the Philippines such request is not only a religious act but a *social* one, it is believed that to deny such request would be a very rude act. The Compadre System in the private sectors comes in handy in cases of hunting job, seeking money in times of need, the need for transportation vehicles, and the need for medical attendance.

3 THE FILIPINO FAMILY AND KINSHIP

The basic units of the Philippine social organization are the *elementary* family which includes the father, mother, and children, and the *bilateral extended* family which embraces all relatives of the father and the mother. Of special importance is the sibling group, the unit formed by brothers and sisters. There are no clans or similar unilateral kinship groups in the Philippines. The elementary family and the sibling group form the primary bases of corporate action.

The Philippine society may be characterized as *familial*. This means that the influence of kinship, which centers on the family, is far-reaching. The persuasive influence of the family upon all segments of Philippine social organization can be illustrated in many ways. Religious responsibility, for example, is familial rather than church-centered. Each home has a family shrine. The large images carried in the community processions during Holy Week are owned and kept by individual families, usually the wealthier ones. Filipino type of family has had a considerable influence on the forms of religious beliefs and activities introduced by organized religions.

The influence of the family upon economic and entrepreneurial business activities is also great. The elementary family is the basic production unit in agricultural activities, cottage industries, gathering, and in local and subsistence fishing. Even among paid agricultural workers two or more members of a family will commonly be found working together. The so-called "corporations" found in urban areas are generally family holdings. Distribution of corporate stock beyond the kin group has not been successful in most cases. The extensive practice of nepotism in the Philippines is thoroughly understandable when the economic solidarity characteristic of family life is considered.

The fragmented character of the *larger* Philippine society is a result, in part, of the Filipino type of family and kinship structure. The prevailing family structure emphasizes loyalty and support of the family, not of any higher level of social organization. In the barrio, political organizations and group activities are organized in terms of kinship and by common economic and ritual interests. One or more families form the core of these group activities, the leadership usually being provided by the dominant family or families. Wealth and the size of a man's family and kinship group are the primary determinants of leadership. The resulting familial orientation is centripetal, making for highly segmented communities and an almost complete lack of legal self-government. It is understandable, therefore, why government and municipal programs have found so little real support in the typical barrio.

The role of the family in the Philippines, as actually received by Filipinos, is explicitly stated in the new Civil Code of the Philippines (1953). Article number 216 states: "The family is a basic social institution which public policy cherishes and protects." And in Article number 220:

In case of doubt, all presumptions favor the solidarity of the family. Thus, every intendment (understanding) of law of fact leans toward the validity of marriage, the indissolubility of the marriage bond, the legitimacy of children, the community of property during the marriage, the authority of parents over their children, and the validity of the defense for any member of the family in cases of unlawful aggression.

A further look into the structure of the Filipino family shows the following:

1. The Filipino family is the nuclear unit around which social activities are organized—it is the basic unit of corporate action.

2. The interests of the individual in Philippine society are secondary to those of the family. In some areas of the Philippines, marriages are arranged by the parents; children were often pledged when they were very young. Marriage is an alliance of two families. The payment of a dowry by the groom and his relatives to the parents of the bride, which is practised even in

39

some Christian areas, stands as a symbol of alignment of the two families and of the reciprocal obligations incurred by marriage. Even in big cities, the Filipino parents, as well as older relatives, exert great influence in the choice of spouses by their children.

3. Marriage is viewed as a permanent contract, an "inviolable social institution." (Civil Code No. 14). Divorce is not recognized in the Philippines, although legal separation is permitted in cases of adultery, and when one spouse attempts to take the life of the other.

4. An offense against one member of the family is perceived as a threat to the whole family. An unlawful or immoral act committed by one family member brings discredit to every family member. However, the family cherishes and protects transgressors as a family member, even though the misdeed is not condoned, and any remark by a non-relative reflecting upon the behavior of the wayward member is considered a serious offense against the entire family.

5. Familial ties are not broken by marriage, distance of residence, or by a change in the social status of a family member. If a Filipino gets married and has substantial income, he is obliged to continue supporting his brothers and sisters. If a boy from a barrio has found a successful position in Manila, he is expected to continue to help his family. Furthermore, he is expected to return home to participate in family gatherings, like fiestas, despite the distance involved.

6. Custom and the new Civil Code provide for mutual support among members of the family. If a man is in a position to hire a kinsman, he will do so. To abandon or ignore the plight of a family member reflects dishonorably on that family. Thus, institutions such as "Home for the Aged" are rare, the family generally assuming these responsibilities. Children are duty-bound to support parents in their old age, and even illegitimate children become an integral part of the family.

7. As a rule the residence of a family is with the paternal kin that is near or in the barrio of the parents of the husband. The actual residence of a married couple is determined, however, by a number of variables: the location and relative amount of the land which the two bring to marriage; their respective number of siblings; and the extent of intra-village marriage. If the girl is the only child and has land, while the boy has many brothers and sisters and very little land, residence may be near

40

the parents of the girl.

8. The typical composition of the Filipino household is one elementary family with the addition of one or more close relatives, usually the widowed parents, unmarried siblings, or members of the family abandoned by their spouses.

9. Though marriage forms a new "family of procreation," the husband and wife are still integral parts of their respective "families of orientation." Thus, if a husband abuses his wife, her kinsmen will intervene, for she is still a member of her natal group.

10. The Filipino family is externally patriarchical but internally matriarchical. The mother plays a very active role in the family, such as sharing agricultural and business duties and responsibilities, assuming the religious obligations of the family and doing the household chores. The active role of the Filipino woman as the mother of a family is facilitated by the frequent presence of older women or siblings in the household who care for the younger children.

11. The separation of the sexes is emphasized in the family. Young women are confined to the home and taught to hide and control their emotions and thoughts. They are carefully chaperoned when with the opposite sex. Before and after marriage, a display of affection in public between husband and wife is looked down upon.

12. Authority is not based simply on sex but on *age*. Philippine society is influenced by the opinions of all individuals, regardless of sex, older than one self. Thus, authority is invested not simply in the father and mother but in parents and in grandparents as well. It is specifically stated in the New Civil Code that ". . . grandparents should be consulted by all members of the family on important family questions."

13. The oldest brother or sister in the family has authority over younger siblings, including the right to punish them. When the parents die, the eldest sibling assumes the responsibility for the sibling group. The pattern of generational respect is found in the terminology of address, children speaking to their parents and older persons in the plural form of the second person, that is, by saying *kayo* (plural) not *ikaw* (singular) for *you*.

14. Filipino family life centers on the children.[8] The elementary family is formalized and becomes a structural unit when a child is born to a couple, for unlike his or her parents, the child is related equally to the maternal and paternal kin. The birth of

a child forms a link between the families. Land and other properties are thought of as being held in trusteeship by parents for the children. Family funds are rarely, if ever, spent by the parents for their own wants. On the contrary, the family will plunge into debt for children—for their education, in cases of illness, or for the costume of a daughter who has been chosen queen for the barrio fiesta. Family capital and savings are the inheritance of children, to be divided equally among them. A common excuse for denying loans, even to relatives, is that the properties and money belong to the children, usually the youngest, despite the relatively firm pattern of authority. The relationship between alternating generations, grandparents and grandchildren is often very close and affectionate. Although the grandparents are in an authoritative position, they rarely discipline children. A child who has been raised by grandparents is often thought of as a "spoiled child."

15. Family relationship is extended to distant cousins, who are given help if needed. The usual residential pattern is based on kinship which reinforces the unity of extended families. If large, as well as localized, they can be powerful and influential. Politics in local areas is often controlled by large, wealthy families. The selection of the barrio captain, for example, is made on the basis of his representing a dominant kin group.

16. Following marriage, the Filipino's ties, duties and obligations are predominantly to the family and kin group, both consanguineous and affine. There is relatively little time for "friendship" and when it does develop, the mechanism of ritual kinships of *compadrazco* (ritual co-parenthood) are employed to formalize the relationship.

17. Relationships within the bounds of kinship are relatively secure and predictable. Conversely, a marked social distance generally separates members of a kin group from all non-kinsmen.

18. Comparing the Filipino social system with the Western social system, the former puts much stress on the collective body. The individual finds fulfillment as a person in the family-neighborhood type milieu. The family is the center of society. Everything revolves around the relationships existing between the persons within the family structure. The neighborhood-type center is where the individuals *collectively* seek support. The collectivization of persons places stress on the group as means of

socialization. Every individual then is classified, so to speak, within a tight, immobile strata performing the roles and functions in accordance with the established structure.

The Western social system lays emphasis on the individual as an individual. The individual is the Western society. Society works for the benefit of the person in such ways that personal interests, needs and wants are secured and protected. A person, in a sense, chooses for himself his own function and role. The Western man lives within a mobile strata which is not tightly centered around family-neighborhood relationships. The Filipino social system, on the other hand, is inflexible. The family is the Filipino society. The family chooses for the individual his own function and role.

The Father in the Filipino Family

The father-husband is the head of the family and implicitly obeyed by wife and children. He has the duty of meeting the financial needs of the family. A typical Filipino husband hands his income almost intact to his wife and she takes care of budgeting the family funds. Lately, many wives have taken on paying jobs, easing their husbands of the load of providing for the family as well as bringing in additional income.

The Filipino husband is usually excused from the petty details of housekeeping such as dishwashing, floor husking, yard sweeping or house cleaning. The more strenuous jobs are allotted to him, such as planting, wood chopping, or pounding palay.

The Filipino father is the main source of discipline in the family and he uses corporal punishment on both son and daughter. For the Westerners this would seem cruelty to children. With the younger children, the father is a sort of bogeyman used as a threat by the mother to bring the children to behave themselves.

The Mother in the Filipino Family

The mother-wife takes care of the thousand and one little details of living and loving to form a cohesive, unified family unit. She concerns herself with the planning of the daily menus or paying the salary of the maids. She is in charge of the home and all details pertaining to the children, such as seeing them fed, clothed, and ready for school.

The Filipino mother-wife, as a shrewd bargain hunter, will spend an extra hour in the market to cut her marketing expenses by a few centavos.

Strange as it may seem, the Filipino wife is the equal of her man. Unlike her Oriental counterparts, she occupies high positions in the family and society. The Filipino woman has regained most of her traditional rights and capacities under the New Civil Code, Republic Act No. 386. The New Civil Code allows the woman to transact business without the prior consent of her husband and to dispose of property which she brought to marriage. The Filipino woman now enjoys the same educational privileges and suffrage rights as her husband. Under the old Civil Code, the husband could alienate conjugal property without his wife's knowledge or consent. At present, without his wife's consent the husband cannot do so.

The dedication a Filipino wife could give her husband is proverbial. But woe to him if he commits conjugal infidelity. Even the most sophisticated and educated Filipino wife is not above undignified hair-pulling, biting and scratching. Yet the Filipino wife is most practical and will forgive in order "to save face." She will go to absurd lengths to protect her family and her children.[9]

The Children in the Filipino Family

To the Westerner, the Filipino child appears to be pampered because of his prolonged childhood during which he is absolved from adult responsibility. He is not rushed toward adult responsibilities and expectations are kept below the child's potential.

The care and affection lavished upon him in his childhood builds up the clannish feeling of belonging which is ingrained in the Filipino child unto his adult days. As a result, he stands up for the family against all adversities.

The Filipino child has a right to an education. The Revised Civil Code provides for an education "in keeping with their (the parents') means." Filipino parents go into all sorts of sacrifice to provide the highest educational opportunities for their children. The children are some kind of insurance for the future, and even when there is no need to contribute to the parent's support, the moral obligation to give financial help is still there.

"Blood is thicker than water" applies to the Filipino family. A sibling will support a wastrel brother, even against the wishes of his wife, surreptitiously, if necessary. A financially successful sibling will take on as his obligation the providing of better jobs for his less fortunate relatives. This explains the proliferation of vice-presidencies in family corporations, as well as nepotism in public office.

Unlike the child who is brought up in a Western culture, the Filipino child is usually expected to accept parental control because they brought him into this world. Furthermore, the Filipino child, for training purposes and for family convenience, is gradually initiated into running errands, caring for younger siblings, doing household chores and feeding domestic animals. To discipline the child, Filipino mothers use physical punishments, slaps and spanking, pinching, beating, ear-pulling frequently. Scolding and haranguing are also common. This might scandalize a Westerner who disciplines her child by deprivation of privileges. In contrast to the Western child who is usually only required to obey his parents and occasionally an older sibling, the Filipino child must obey many other people—his older siblings and relatives, as well as parents. Western mothers expect obedience from their children without delay. Filipino parents use teasing to wheedle the child into obeying.

Births

Filipinos usually give a warm welcome to a new-born baby in the family. They will responsibly care and rear him with loving and tender care. Emotional support, affectionate touching and close physical contact are abudantly given to a Filipino baby not only by the mother and father but also by the grandparents, brothers, sisters and relatives.

Because of superstitious beliefs, Filipino parents observe many restrictions while waiting for the birth of their baby. Today, many Filipino parents go to the hospital to deliver their babies, but rural Filipinos prefer to have the child at home with the services of a midwife.

In spite of intensive and extensive family planning campaigns

45

held in the country, the large family norm still persists among Filipino parents. Four basic considerations seem to motivate Filipino couples to continue having large families.[10]

1. Children are looked upon as economic assets rather than liabilities. They are considered future contributors to the family income and as "social security" during old age of the parents.

2. Children are considered signs of God's blessings. That is, the more children a couple has, the more they are blessed. Couples who have fewer children are said to be unfortunate; it is sometimes interpreted to mean they are being punished by God.

3. Children bring happiness to parents, siblings and other relatives. As the saying goes, "the more the merrier."

4. Children are considered public evidences of such attributes as maleness among men and fulfillment of motherhood among women.

Mothers are not given gifts on the birth of a baby, but, for the baby, little outfits, dresses or blankets are appreciated. There is no rule about the number or color of gifts though cheerful, bright or pastel colors are in good taste. Visits may be made any-time after the first day of delivery of the baby.

Young boys are usually circumcised when they reach puberty although this operation which consists of cutting the foreskin covering the top part of the penis can be undergone soon after birth or between eight and twelve years of age. The operation may be done not necessarily by a doctor. In rural areas, several boys may have the operation together by a local medicine man with crude methods. For Filipino males circumcision is a rite that celebrates the passage of the boy from childhood to manhood so much so that if a young man is found uncircumcised the other males consider him as effeminate. In ten or twelve days the young man is completely healed and he rejoices that he has "passed the test" and taken his first step into the world of man-hood.

Female circumcision or clitoridectomy (an operation which consists of removing the foreskin covering the clitoris) is not widely practiced in the Philippines. There are some clinics in Manila that do the operation but Filipino women are by nature shy and conservative on this matter.

46

The Filipino Youth

"East is East and West is West, said Old Man Kipling, and never the twain shall meet." But Filipino youth are riddling the body of Kipling with cultural bullets. Filipino youth's language is a heady brew of American slang and vernacular teenage jargon: "bread" means "money"; "jingle" means "passing water"; "chicks" means "girls" and "cats" means "boys."

To a Western observer, the Filipino teener is like his average American counterpart. He dances the current dance steps and sings the current pop hits. Nevertheless, if one digs deeper he will find that the Filipino youth is still a product of his own Filipino environment and influences. The following chart depicts the influences that act upon the Filipino child and the Filipino adult that comes out as a result of the experiences in the process of child rearing as practiced in the country.[11]

The Filipino Child Influences	The Filipino Youth Characteristics
Child rearing practices, cultural patterns	Modesty
Extended family	Politeness
Close family ties	Gentleness
Gentleness	Friendliness
Permissiveness	Loyalty
Religious background	Hospitality
Feeding and weaning practices	Love of music and dancing
Suppression of hostility	Personal cleanliness
Many figures of identification	Kindness
Protection	Respect for elders
Emphasis on early development	Amor propio (sensitive ego)
Teasing	Bahala na ("Leave it to fate")
Spanking	Ningas cogon (Lack of persistence)
Responsibility for younger siblings	Mañana habit (procrastination)
Authoritarian parents	Imitation
Yayas (nursemaid)	Inferiority
Intrusiveness	Extravagance
Breaking the will	Persistence of old beliefs
Bayanihan (working together)	Non-interference (indifference)
	Competitiveness
	Dependency
	Irresponsibility
	Lack of discipline
	Hiya

From these influences and characteristics of the Filipino youth we can identify the following patterns of behavior:

1. The Filipino youth is friendly, hospitable and sensitive. These traits are sometimes carried to an extreme. Hospitality for instance, may include feeling insulted if a guest does not partake of the food or meals offered to him. Friendliness and courtesy may extend to agreeing with the other person even without real conviction. Oversensitivity to criticism and loss of face may lead to brooding, and later, violence. Aggressiveness is suppressed very strongly, but may be released explosively when the person becomes "full."[12]

2. The Filipino youth likes group work and offers help freely to friends or neighbors needing help. Work for others is done cheerfully and without expectation of payment except for a free meal or merienda.

3. The Filipino youth has great respect for age and for parents. He hesitates to question authority. In certain matters, he may be right but he has to defer, at least temporarily, to an older person who may be wrong.

4. The Filipino youth are usually given what they ask for. Some become "spoiled."

5. The Filipino youth are dependent on parents for a long time particularly in matters requiring decisions. At times he may not even be prepared to make decisions regarding the clothes he will wear to school. He does not know how to handle allowance money. To approach a teacher or a professor, he needs to have somebody accompany him.

6. The Filipino youth is closely attached to his family and his friends. He finds difficulty when he loses these emotional props. He needs to be part of a group or a gang.

7. The Filipino youth is expected to live up to the family expectation. The parents may choose his course for him even if he is not sure that it is what he wants. The family's traditions and values may dictate that the student take a course unsuited to him. In the Philippines, there is a high value placed on prestigious careers such as medicine and law.

8. The Filipino youth exposed to urban culture tends to consider his parents and the older generation in general, as old-fashioned. He resents their restrictions on matters of dating, taking trips, choice of clothes, allowance, and choice of friends

and resent their invasion of his privacy. The females may resent being chaperoned and being restricted on the use of cosmetics.

9. The Filipino youth has a great fear of displeasing a figure of authority or offending a person he considers important.

10. The Filipino youth's culture is a "shame" culture rather than a "guilt" culture. Many of his actions are motivated by the desire to conform and to avoid shame or disgrace. His behavior is controlled by fear of censure. Regulation comes from the outside rather than inside.

The Filipino Woman

During the pre-Hispanic or barangay culture, the Filipino woman was pretty much the queen in the house. The husband, who was usually a warrior, let his woman have her way. Presently, the Filipino woman is still master of the house, or she is made to feel that way.[13]

The phrase "under the saya" (under the skirt) is the Filipino male's admission that the woman wears the pants in the house, or if she doesn't, she selects what pair of pants her man will wear. The Filipino woman managed the purse at home during the barangay era and by virtue of this acquired a measure of power in business affairs. The Filipino woman has more rights than her cousins in other Asian countries. In the Philippines, Filipino women are very active and frequently more aggressive than men in social and economic activities. It is said that women in the Philippines are like inclement weekend weather. They are to be talked about but not dealt with. They are unforecastably bright, cloudy, windy, and quite monsoonish if one says one bad word about them.

The Filipino woman belongs to the weaker sex and even if she has never been really helpless, she is smart enough to look incapable in order to be best attended to by the men. The Filipino woman is smart: she knows how to swoon prettily, how to drop handkherchiefs and eyelids effectively and how to appear dependent and naive. She can put a façade of discretion, humility, graciousness, sweetness, docility, meekness and remarkable beauty hiding a wealth of intelligence, strength, willfulness, determination, shrewdness and enterprise. Here lies the differences between the Filipino women and the women of the

Western World. Filipino women have mastered the art of hiding their stronger qualities underneath the softer ones.

In the present times when the modern Filipina is so highly education-conscious she begins to emerge into the open to compete in all the fields of endeavor. In the Philippines, the female population accounts for 82 percent of the literate population as against 84-86 percent for the males.

Historians say that before the advent of the Spaniards, women of the Philippines enjoyed equal rights with men—daughters could succeed to the headship of the barangay (at least two noted women rulers are named, Queen Sima and Princess Urduja) and could become priestesses. The Filipino legend on the origin of the human race, unlike the biblical version of Eve coming from Adam's rib, has man and woman simultaneously emerging from a huge bamboo. That was equality to begin with.

In the Filipino family, the wife holds the purse, husbands hand over their check (pay) and get an allowance in return and the wife manages the affairs of the household. Filipino women are expected to possess kindness and tolerance, spirituality or humaneness. In the Philippines, strange powers of women over which men have no control are depicted in the *aswangs*, the *mangkukulam*, and the *manananggal*. These are witches and half-bodied women supposed to be flying at night. Filipino women have a distaste for pornography because sex for them has a sacred and mysterious meaning. They value sex as part of a genuine loving relationship.

4 ETHICAL AND NORMATIVE BEHAVIOR OF FILIPINOS

Ethics bases itself on what is human. Not everything is universal in human nature. As Clyde Kluckholm and Henry A. Murray say "Every man is in certain respects (a) like all other men. (b) like some other men, (c) like no other man."[14] It is within the context of (b) that ethical and normative behavior of people in the Philippines has its distinctive characteristics.

Culture shapes the perception of its members. Culture means the system of symbols and meanings people use to organize their ideas, interpret their experiences, make decisions, and ultimately guide their actions. Considering the Filipino cultural orientation reveals three main traits which highlight Filipino behavior and decision-making. These are *personalism, familism,* and *particularism* (or *popularism*).

According to a Filipino anthropologist personalism has to do with the degree of emphasis Filipinos give to interpersonal relations or to face-to-face encounters.[15] The rule of social and cultural activities emphasizes personalized techniques of doing things. Successful leadership must have a tinge of personal touch. Problem-solving is effective if handled through good personal relations rather than group deliberation, debate and collegial reasoning. Communication has difficulty flowing through channels unless personally attended to by the person concerned.

Familism, on the other hand, gives emphasis on the welfare and interest of the family over the welfare and interest of the community. The family is the basis of group action. Almost all activities in the community center on the family. Within the neighborhood, it is the family, not the individual members,

51

which decide on the resolution of important matters. The interest of the family is primary to that of the individual members composing it. The pervasive influence of the family on individual and group behavior, as reinforced by the highly personalistic emphasis on social interactions, gives rise to heightened emphasis on particularistic tendencies. Each individual appears to strive hard to promote his own and his family's interests over the larger community interests. To be popular is the highest compliment a Filipino can receive from his kinsmen, neighbors and acquaintances. Conformity to codes of proper conduct is rewarded with cooperation and assistance and non-conformity is punished by withdrawal of support.

This outlook in life and action is influenced by the child-rearing practices in the Philippines. A study of cross-cultural child-rearing practices shows how personalities are formed according to one's culture. The following shows the contrasts between the American and the Filipino child:[16]

CONTRASTS BETWEEN FILIPINO AND AMERICAN CHILD-REARING PRACTICES

Filipino	*American*
1. Born in a personalized environment. Baby is breast-fed and often touched by members of the family.	1. Born in an impersonal environment. Baby is rarely breast-fed.
2. *Sakop* (In-group) stressed; child must conform with the rest. Individuality discouraged. Mothers discourage early attempts of child to walk.	2. Individuality and uniqueness stressed. Child is consulted on what he likes. Mothers encourage early attempts of child to walk.
3. Privacy not stressed; infant never left alone.	3. Privacy stressed. Child learns and values to be alone and independent.
4. Learns to respect older siblings and authority. Parents are authoritarian.	4. Learns to be egalitarian. Parents are democratic.
5. Mothers stress harmony and less competition. Child learns to respect the feelings of others.	5. Mothers encourage their children to compete with each other. Child learns to be insensitive to feelings of others.

Mechanism used: teasing

Mechanism used: personal ambition, competition which often leads to hostility.

Result: shame orientation; success and failure are not personal but sakop-oriented.

Result: guilt orientation; stress on personal success and failure.

6. Parents promise a lot; when promises are broken, the child learns not to be disappointed.

6. Parents are reluctant in making promises which they cannot keep. Child disappointed on broken promises.

The foregoing contrasts between American and Filipino child-rearing practices illustrate how culture influences the ethical and normative behavior of its members. This can be diagrammed as follows:[7]

American Cultural Orientation　　　　　*Filipino Cultural Orientation*

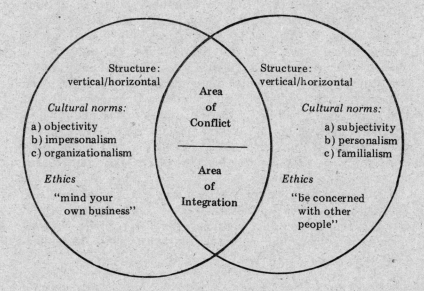

Structure: vertical/horizontal

Cultural norms:
a) objectivity
b) impersonalism
c) organizationalism

Ethics
"mind your own business"

Area of Conflict

Area of Integration

Structure: vertical/horizontal

Cultural norms:
a) subjectivity
b) personalism
c) familialism

Ethics
"be concerned with other people"

Filipino Normative Environment

The Filipino cultural orientation is supported by shared values which function as the basis of shared behavior common to most Filipinos. Values have reference to standards people use for evaluating what is right or wrong, good or evil. Values are related to norms which are rules of conduct specific to given social situations.

The Filipino has two sets of paradoxical traits and patterns of relationship that are imbued by his culture. The first set is the highly structured and authoritarian familial set-up where roles are prescribed especially for younger members of the family. This is characterized by autocratic leadership of the elder-members, submitting one's self to the decision of the family elders, and almost one-way communication in the pecking order. The second set of social relationship that the Filipino has, which ironically exists side by side with the highly structured set-up, is the strong communitarian practice called *Bayanihan* which literally means "being a hero." This practice ignores social ranking, structures, leadership roles and authority relationships. The roles in the structured set-up mentioned earlier cease to exist. Surprisingly, the Filipino is at home with both cultural practices in his social life. He shifts from one setting to another with unbelievable ease and grace. In the first set-up there is no way that a child can lead the elders in any form of decision-making. In the Bayanihan set-up, however, if a child proves that he has the right qualification needed for the task, he may lead the elders, not excluding his father and elder brothers.

There are three main imperatives that underlie Filipino value orientation: relational imperatives, emotional imperatives and moral imperatives (see diagram below).[18] Taken altogether, they make up the whole Filipino normative environment. The imperatives are the following:

Relational imperatives—This refers to the emphasis given by Filipinos to the actual person-to-person encounters. Present to a Filipino and a Westerner this problem:

On a sea voyage, you are traveling with your wife, your child, and your mother. The ship begins to sink. Of your family, you are the only one who can swim—and you can only save one other individual. Whom do you save? A Westerner will tend to opt to

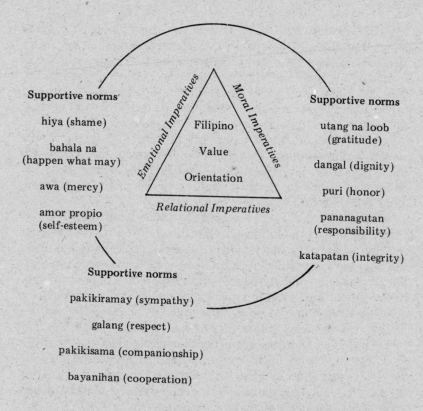

Supportive norms

hiya (shame)

bahala na
(happen what may)

awa (mercy)

amor propio
(self-esteem)

Emotional Imperatives

Filipino

Value

Orientation

Moral Imperatives

Relational Imperatives

Supportive norms

utang na loob
(gratitude)

dangal (dignity)

puri (honor)

pananagutan
(responsibility)

katapatan (integrity)

Supportive norms

pakikiramay (sympathy)

galang (respect)

pakikisama (companionship)

bayanihan (cooperation)

save the child or the wife but not the mother. A Filipino very likely will choose to save the mother. The rationale is that you can always remarry and have more children, but you cannot have another mother. Family runs the Filipino's life. His experience of self is totally linked with his relationship with people who are important to him. His ties with friends or kin color his perceptions and influence his life goals and even determine his daily activities. On the basis of these ties, he chooses a career, a place to live in and even a wife. To preserve these ties, he conforms, he compromises, and sometimes cheats.

The Westerner is less affected by the interpersonal ties for he has few of these. He takes pride in being independent and self-sufficient and sees no necessity to consider family in making his decisions. He, therefore, tends to see the Filipino as weak and dependent, imprisoned by his relationships. The Filipino, in turn, is shocked by the Westerner's coldness and hard-heartedness.

The Western man is an individual. The Filipino is a social man—a family man. The Westerner operates in a much less stratified society. When the Westerner speaks of his family, he generally means his wife and children. But the term "family," to the Filipino, embraces a wider social system, for it includes not only his wife and children but also his parents, grandparents, in-laws, and sometimes it extends to friends and associates.

The Westerner, many times, has no family to speak of. His so-called aggressiveness, therefore, proceeds from his recognition that ultimately he is alone, that after some time, when his children have grown, he must fend for himself. This fear of being alone is alien to the Filipino psyche.

The Filipino does not regard the depersonalized organizational scheme as the definition of rational order. What is rational for him is the intimately human personalistic transaction. Thus the Filipino's dependency on authority or conversely, the hesitancy to accept individual responsibility. The Filipino worker, for example, prefers group-centered activity that is directed by a strong authoritarian leader, most probably an outgrowth of the family-centered cultural tradition. He tends to place a much higher value on the need for affiliation rather than the need for achievement. He is much more personal in his worldview and somewhat less objective than his Western counterpart. He is more hesitant to be held responsible for decisions or to be individually identified in the decision making process.

This personal relation is emphasized by the following Filipino values:

1. *Pakikiramay* or going out of one's way to assist even without being asked.

2. *Pakikisama* or going along with certain people whom one may like to displease for various reasons.

3. *Bayanihan* or being a hero by giving assistance without compensation.

4. *Paggalang* or giving respect to the opinions of those who are elders, in authority or of peers during deliberations of important matters.

Emotional imperatives—Supporting the relational imperatives are emotionally-laden norms. The Filipino's uncontrollable reaction to anything done which he considers an affront to his honor, dignity, and pride, is reflective of the way he structures his personal relations, how he looks at himself relative to another individual. A harsh speech or a discourteous comment is enough to trigger a violent reaction from a Filipino. Take the case of an expatriate who scolds his Filipino subordinate because he cannot fully comprehend a technical process. The Filipino subordinate will surely be *mapapahiya* (embarrassed) with his circle of friends. Furthermore, the expatriate can say a lot of other things (with good intentions) which can cause undue embarrassment. This will definitely cause a gap between the Filipino subordinate and his Western boss. Consequently, this becomes a deterrent to harmonious working and productivity. Furthermore, when intense conflict is induced, there might even be sabotage of each other's performance, back-talking or physical injury. A Filipino would prefer not to disagree than take the risk of being offended. However, when offended he goes into a frenzied attack, physically or verbally.

When a Westerner's personal rights are trampled upon, his first reaction is ordinarily to complain and fight back. The Filipino is surprised to see Westerners quarrel over disagreements on personal rights and afterwards become friends as if nothing happened at all. This is because the Filipino has been culturally brought up to value harmony. If a Filipino's rights are trampled upon, he first uses the friendly way. He often makes his feelings known through the indirect or roundabout approach. For him to directly confront someone will have lasting wounds which no amount of friendly reconciliation can heal. Only after the friendly means (pakikisama) are exhausted does he resort to violence (*pakikibaka*).

The Filipino desire for harmony does not mean the absence of actual conflict. Truly enough, for him violence or a direct confrontation is not the first step. However, if put to shame, the Filipino can turn violent. Any attempt at casting doubt upon or questioning a Filipino's action, integrity and honor even if it is true can elicit vindictive reaction from him. One who publicly denounces a Filipino may only get worse results because he did not follow the cultural norm of first airing grievances privately and politely.

The average Westerner conducts his personal life and his maintenance of law and order in the community on principles of right or wrong; the average Filipino, on sanctions of shame, dishonor, ridicule, or impropriety. The average Westerner is forced to categorize his conduct in universal impersonal terms. The "law is the law" and "right is right," regardless of other considerations. The average Filipino takes the law from the concrete and personal angle. He has a shame culture and this factor greatly affects his behavior. A Filipino feels that saving his honor is more important than the truth. The Westerner's passion for the truth no matter who is hurt is illustrated in exposing the misdeeds of the departed. But this is not the case for the Filipino. Any prominent official's misdeeds are buried with him; his memory is honored for he has gone.

Take the case of the concept of justice. Justice for the Filipino is not something abstract. Being just is something concrete, visible; someone from whom you can elicit sympathy or pity. Justice is the policeman, the judge, the teacher, the principal, the dean, the boss, the employer. The ethics of justice for the Filipino is based on the value of harmony. Justice for Filipino is not individualistic but communitarian. The individualistic model of justice is quite strong for the Westerners, particularly the Americans. An American descendant of second or third generation immigrants, for example, who still does menial jobs such as ditchdigging is looked down upon. The normal American reaction is: "What is the matter? He's not getting ahead." Personal dignity is therefore measured in terms of an exterior, economic standard. On the other hand, the Filipino's idea of personal dignity is not exterior but interior. The external differences are not the ultimate norm of personal dignity. The Filipino is not worried where he belongs in the community. His dignity is in his "self." A manifestation of this sense of dignity is his unwillingness to be put to shame. The Filipino is aware of his self-dignity even if he may be externally poor, even if he wears rags or his house may be of nipa and bamboo. The Filipino's concept of justice is "inner self-worth," not necessarily equality to all.

Moral imperatives—According to Dr. F. Landa Jocano, Filipinos, if viewed from within the culture, are more moralistic than ordinarily perceived. Moral values continuously influence Filipino behavior. Filipinos are keen in observing the moral undertones of their actions.

The most powerful moral imperative in Filipino culture is *utang na loob* or the debt of gratitude. This debt of gratitude,

58

loyalty or commitment is strongly related to the value of sakop or in-group. The sakop can be a person's peers, townmates, class-mates, relatives, officemates, etc. The mechanisms for sakop-making are closeness of living, ritual kinship such as in baptism, marriage, ordination, investitures or in similar inaugurations as the blessings of a new house. The sakop prevails over the individual. It demands from the individual a continuing act of reciprocal action with the fellow members. The Filipino as an individual finds fulfillment in sakop-fulfillment.

Interpersonalism and hierarchy are the two characteristics of the sakop. Issues do not matter; it is personal allegiance to the head that matters. Degrees of disparity in age such as among brothers and sisters where being the eldest, second to the eldest, and so on, matters a lot. Thus in Philippine culture, age is equated to wisdom and experience that is, the elder is considered more authoritative. The sakop stresses ranking. To a Filipino inequalities based on hereditary status or special privilege is normal and acceptable; to a Westerner this is shocking and un-acceptable. This hierarchic character of the sakop has a bearing on the concept of responsibility and imputability. When an en-deavor fails, the Filipino does not blame himself but his sakop. The imputability is more sakop-oriented. Just as in the Filipino family, the older sibling is responsible for the acts of his younger siblings, the sakop head assumes more of the responsibility for the sakop's failure.

The sakop nature is reflected on the concept of property. In the Western individualist orientation, the ethics of private property has also an individualistic tone. In the Filipino sakop-orientation, private property has a communitarian tone. In a community where there are Filipinos and there exists a sakop feeling, private property is community's property. If a person happens to own an electric iron or the only automobile in that community, the other sakop members feel that they have a right to that electric iron or automobile. If the person does not allow the other members to use it, then he has broken the moral im-perative of the sakop.

The sharing of goods in the sakop dimension might actually be "borrowing." The Filipinos, for example, who have a strong sense of sakop property, consider things "borrowed" what Westerners consider "stealing." Getting fruits in somebody's yard without permission from a neighbor is not always stealing

59

when it is to help oneself. If property is held c··mmon in a family, there is no "stealing" in the sakop just as there is no stealing in a closely-knit family. The person who got the fruit, however, should have the intention of reciprocating the favor given by the owner of the yard.

The Filipino abhors the person who thinks independently from the sakop. This is because his form of thinking is holistic and concrete. Unlike the Westerner, he cannot hate the sin but love the sinner. Persons as concrete phenomena take precedence to abstract and impersonal concepts or values. The typical Filipino's thinking and feeling go together. He uses truth diplomatically in order to preserve rapport with people. Truth is delivered indirectly, among intimates through teasing or *biruan*. It is teasing if it misses, it is true if it hits the person for whom it was intended.

Another way of indirectly delivering the truth is through *parinig*, that is, letting the intended party hear by speaking to a different person. For the Westerner truth is characterized by the either-or-alternative; for the Filipino it is both-and. Westerners value truth *above* person; Filipinos value truth *and* person. This is because the Filipino has a shame culture and this factor greatly affects his behavior. For him, the moral imperative is "truth in charity." Some Western cultures expect a straight answer—even if the truth hurts; the Filipino culture demands that one should wait for the right moment and the use of euphemisms and roundabout ways in telling the truth. Oftentimes the truth as an answer is limited to allusions in the hope that the person concerned would get the message.

The Westerner is concerned with the *what* of the truth, the Filipino, with the *how*, *when* and *who* says the truth. Thus, in the Filipino culture, when a person's honor is at stake, he is allowed not to tell the truth in order to save his face. Sakop and family members are allowed not to tell the truth in order to protect the sakop and family honor. Since the value of person is higher than the value of truth in the Filipino culture, parents can hide truth from their children for the good of the latter.

Promises and vows in the Filipino context assume sakop dimensions. Filipino children feel obliged to fulfill promises or vows done by their parents. A Filipino father who promises to go to Antipolo Church (a shrine in the Philippines) yearly every May may have his promise fulfilled in the person of his son.

60

Women in the Philippines

Unlike in other Asian countries women in the Philippines occupy a high status. As a wife the Filipino woman holds the purse and manages the affairs of the household. Married women are permitted to work in many fields. They carry their talents from the home to where the economic activity is.

Equality with men is a birthright of the Filipino women. Unlike her Western sisters, they didn't have to march the streets to be heard. Philippine literature alone presages the simultaneous nascence of the sexes. The most popular tale of creation relates how the first man and woman came from the bamboo tree. A *tikling* bird pecked at the bamboo until it split; from the same bamboo cylinder sprang Malakas (the Strong) and Maganda (the Beautiful). Discovering their compatible natures, they moved toward their assigned roles and without guilt or grandeur populated the entire country.

The new Philippine Constitution provides equal opportunities in employment regardless of sex. It amends and expands the legal rights of women and clearly defines the status of married women. Under the family law, the Filipina wife assumes management of domestic affairs. She may purchase things necessary for the support of the family and even borrow money for this purpose should circumstance dictate. Although the husband is named administrator of conjugal properties, the wife who is co-owner, may for cause, exercise this power. With few exceptions, the husband may not dispose of real properties without the wife's consent.

In the new Constitution marriage to an alien does not strip the Filipino woman of her Philippine citizenship, unless through her own act or omission, she is deemed to have renounced such citizenship. Her children are considered natural-born citizens of the Philippines by virtue of her own citizenship.

Women are highly respected in the Philippines. They may walk alone on the streets. They can also drive alone. Western women, however, are expected to dress discreetly and modestly; this is because their white complexion tends to attract much attention of the men.

Some Guidelines for Women:

Below are some *don'ts* for women to avoid getting into trouble:

1. A woman should not try to look elegant by looking haughty. If she does this, she is on the wrong track using the wrong trick. Instead of causing heads to turn in admiration, she might end up in trouble.

2. She should not wear any kind of clothes she just takes a fancy at. She should consider the place she is going to. There are some places in the Philippines wherein walking in shorts may be an invitation to trouble.

3. She should not be infuriated when men stare or whistle at her. Filipino men show their admiration that way. The most the woman can do is ignore such stare or whistle.

4. She should not act like a man if she wants men to serve her or do a favor for her. She can get what she wants or ask what she needs by using her womanly charms.

5. She should not feel silly sitting passively in a car waiting for her escort to open the door for her. Filipino men love to open car doors for women.

6. Upon hearing gossip whether on politics or of private lives of prominent people, a woman should just let them drop at her feet instead of passing them on.

7. A foreign woman should not isolate herself from other native women. The more she mingles with Filipino women, the easier life in the Philippines will be for her.

8. She should not be embarrassed when asked too personal questions like; "why don't you have children" or "how much rent do you pay?" If she doesn't want to give an answer, she can just smile and change the topic of conversation.

9. She should not drive leisurely in the Philippines. Filipino drivers are not as hospitable on the streets as they are in their homes so the woman driver should drive defensively. Regulations and courtesies are often overlooked by male drivers. Cars and jeepneys dart in and out of traffic lanes and traffic signals are often ignored.

10. She should not be disturbed by the laughter and giggling of Filipinos during embarrassing or emotion-charged situations.

Such behavior does not mean that the incident is being taken lightly.

11. She should not maintain a direct and prolonged eye contacts with Filipinos. This is considered rude.

12. She should not beckon to a Filipino with the index finger for it is considered rude. A downward gesture of the hand is preferably used.

PART TWO

RELATING WITH FILIPINOS

5 COMMUNICATING WITH FILIPINOS

Human communication in a face-to-face situation is almost always complex and frequently interactional. The complexities of motivation and behavior of the sender meets the equal complexities of perception and motivation of the receiver. A variety of impression or messages are sent or received in any effort toward communication, and frequently considerable interaction among the persons involved is necessary for effective communication to take place.

It is important in examining face-to-face communication to recognize some of the forces present in the interpersonal or group situation affecting communication. Communication is not merely by words alone. Tone of voice, choice of words, bodily posture all communicate a variety of messages. Two persons may say, "Good morning," to each other and convey a number of messages. One "Good Morning" may indicate supplication awareness of subordinate status, anxiety as to how the greeting will be received. The other may convey condescension, awareness of power of position, rejection, hostility. Human beings communicate by their behavior as well as by their words alone. Their behavior results from their perception of their own needs to relate to other people and to what they perceive about the actions of others.[19]

To communicate effectively with people of other cultures one has to step back and look at how he develops perception. Meanings are not in words but in people. "Perception" is at the heart of intercultural communication. It is a false assumption to assume that under all circumstances all people think about and

67

perceive the world in basically the same way, and therefore, that whatever one says will mean the same to another. Perceptions play tricks on people. Even though they know intellectually that this is true, in their everyday lives they assume an objectivity and a reliability that is not borne out by events. Things are not always as they seem. They are selective in what they perceive. Most of what are seen, heard, smelled, tasted or felt at any moment is screened out by their conscious minds.

Listening

A high percentage of miscommunication occurs because the listener either isn't listening or is listening to the words, not the meaning. "Active" listening is very important when talking with people from other cultures. A Westerner in his own culture has a dozen little cues which help convey meaning—gestures, facial expressions, body motions, eye contact, voice inflections—all of which in the Westerner occur automatically and are interpreted immediately by him without conscious thought.

In the Philippines, many, if not most, of these non-verbal methods of elaborating and reinforcing the meaning of a verbal message are different. The Westerner has to listen two or three times as hard to Filipinos in order to find out what they really mean. Another way to find out if a Westerner got something straight—if he has "perceived" the message accurately—is to check it out, to ask if something meant what he think it did. Communication is central to building cross-cultural relationships.

The Filipino prefers to use body language rather than words to express itself. Psychologists distinguish between high context and low context cultures.[20] A high context culture possesses mostly information and therefore communication which is internalized in the person or in the physical context. A low context culture, on the other hand, is one in which the majority of the information is contained in the explicit code. Most Westerners' culture is low context. Filipino culture is high context. The Westerner looks for meaning and understanding in what is said; the Filipino in what is not said. The silences for Filipinos together with the pauses between silences are very meaningful. They do convey messages. There is meaning often in the context of Filipinos' silences and pauses.

68

The low context of the Westerner emphasizes sending out or giving accurate messages and in being articulate in so doing. But Filipinos seek mainly to receive messages that often do not have to be stated directly. The Westerner should have in mind the indirectness of the Filipino in contrast to his directness. The Filipino is indirect because he wants to keep his interpersonal encounters pleasant and friendly, because that way the channels of communication will remain open. The Westerner puts a premium on honesty and frankness and feels that communication has to be direct to be effective. Thus, the Westerner is thoroughly baffled by the Filipino who cringes as he encounters the brutally frank Westerner. Filipinos often think, sometimes with good cause, that Westerners are rude and make no attempt to adapt themselves to the manners and customs of their host country. However, when one is ignorant of the fact that such rules exist, one can hardly be blamed for not conforming to them.

A very serious area of stress is the difference in the way Filipinos and Westerners process data—how they come to understand a situation. When a Westerner is talking to somebody, he listens to WHAT the person is saying (to the CONTENT of the speech). To the Filipino, this is less important. When he listens to a person, his immediate instinctive reaction is to try and figure out what the speaker is like, what kind of a person he is, and by identifying with the speaker, he can better understand what he is talking about. An understanding process which relies on "objective" data and one which makes use of identification with the persons involved often can arrive at different interpretations of the same situation.

A good example of Filipino indirectness in communication is the practice of putting up notices on the windshield of the passenger jeepney, a conveyance which is a product of Philippine culture. The jeepney driver, who generally has problems about payment posts the following lines on his windshield: *"God knows Hudas not pay."* HUDAS NOT is the double meaning for "who does not " and Judas the traitor. Another notice runs: *"Upong piso po lamang,"* meaning, please take only one-peso seat. In the Filipino context of communication, this is an advice to all passengers to sit straight, not to occupy more than a sitting space for one so that more passengers can be accommodated.

Among intimates the indirect way of communicating is in the form of teasing or *biruan.* As the Tagalog adage goes, *birubiro kung sanglan, tutoo kung tamaan.* This means that it is teasing if it misses, it is true if it hits. A form of teasing is the Filipino's propensity to giving nicknames. To the Westerner, some nicknames may appear unkind, especially if they are directed at the persons most obvious physical trait. Since childhood, Filipinos are accustomed to name-calling. They have picked up this trait from their schoolmates and playmates. Examples of nicknames are: "Negro" for the dark-colored person, "Insik" or "Sinkit" (slinky eyes) for the Chinese-looking person, "Taba" (stout) for the stout person and "Payat" (thin) for the thin person. The Westerner must note that this making fun, in a teasing way of another person, is a popular pastime in Filipino culture. The person concerned is supposed to prove that he can take it, otherwise he earns another nickname, "pikon" which means one who is touchy or a poor sport.

In Filipino culture, curiosity about another individual's personal life precedes entry into any relationship with him. He likes to describe relationships in terms of similarity to that of his childhood. Thus, in referring to a relationship, one frequently hears remarks such as: "He is like a second father"; She is like an older sister"; "We are just like brothers," "He is like a son to me"; "He is the 'baby' in our class."

In the Philippines, women are inordinately prone to crying. They do not feel embarrassed about crying. The culture allows it as part of their femine nature. Filipino men may shed tears occasionally but in general, crying in men is taken as a sign of weakness. Crying as a form of communication is used in Filipino culture to serve many purposes, from release of unexpressed aggression to creating a guilt feeling in others. It is a way of communicating anger or displeasure.

For Filipinos there are not so many strict taboo areas for discussion. Any subject can be discussed with the Filipino provided the setting is apppropriate. The one exception is anything which will put a Filipino in a situation of being criticized, ridiculed, blamed, or in any way singled out for derogation. The Filipino will naturally not risk being placed in such a position by talking. If, however, he feels pushed to such a spot, the defensive mechanisms to resist may be quite lively, both verbally and behaviorally. The Filipino can be quite adept at using a camouflage of words. Provided he feels safe and secure, the Filipino will talk about anything.

70

On the other hand, the Filipino can play *pakipot* which literally means "to close up," or to play hard to get. A very concrete example of "pakipot" is when a woman who is courted by a man plays hard to get. Even if she loves him she does not say so at once but will take her time in answering him lest she be branded an "easy" girl. Another protective behavior of the Filipino is putting oneself down, or not making the first move towards involvement or commitment. Filipino sayings such as *"Hinihinga ko lang; hindi naman ako nagagalit* (I am merely letting off steam; I am not angry)" or *"Hindi ako mapagtanim, pero masama akong magalit* (I never allow a grudge to take root inside me, but when I get angry, I am terrible)" are some manifestations of this behavior.

Another Filipino trait is *pakitang tao*. This means "showing to others for the benefit of social approval." The Filipino often feels that he is being watched and evaluated whether he be in an office, in the church, in the school or in the community. This leads to subtle posing or playing up to. More often than not a Filipino makes gestures requesting reassurance or "makes *lambing*" (lambing is a Tagalog word that defies accurate translation into English; it is a move to initiate an affectionate exchange). This is a widely accepted cultural practice among Filipino close friends.

Middle or upper class Filipinos communicate in English mixed in varying degrees with Tagalog. Many Filipinos learned English in school and often spoke it ahead of Pilipino. "Tagalized" English is what urban Filipinos in Manila utilize in their daily conversation. The recourse to English is due to the limitations of Tagalog. Tagalog expressions seem to be most deficient in technical terms. In matters regarding sex the Tagalog words seem to be too vulgar.

Filipino English may be further classified into Ilocano English, Pampango English, Waray-waray English, mestizo English, the Ateneo accented English. Some of these Filipino English omits the "h" or pronounces the "f" as "p" or vice-versa. In the Filipino English "Colgate" means toothpaste, "Frigidaire" means refrigerator, "dear" means expensive, "Comfort Room" means restroom, "for awhile" means "one moment please," "I will be the one to" means "I will," "maybe" means "no," "I'll try," "I don't think I can."

6 FILIPINO TRAITS, CUSTOMS AND TRADITIONS

A study of what annoys a person gives a clue to his sense of values and to his character and personality. It is interesting to note what annoy Filipinos for these give an insight into what they value most. The following annoy most Filipinos:

1. Someone who disagrees very strongly with his opinion in a discussion
2. Women smoking in public
3. Fellow Filipinos who put in a foreign accent when speaking
4. A person who looks down on another
5. Foreigners who show complete ignorance about the country
6. Servants who pretend to be of high social status
7. One's putting much attention to very minute details
8. A person who treats another like a servant
9. Criticism from someone who is not his boss
10. Someone telling another how to do his job
11. Inconsideration for another's feelings
12. Racial prejudice in people
13. Body odor
14. A foreigner who always says, "That's the way we do it back home!"
15. Women who dye their hair
16. Being told to hurry up
17. A person with an air of superiority
18. A person who is too brutally frank

19. Rich people who are snobbish
20. Foreigners who write about the Philippines without knowing very much about it
21. People who preach democracy but do not practice it
22. People who demand a definite "yes" or "no" answer

Beneath the above-mentioned annoyances lie what Filipinos value most and some of these are revealed in the three major characteristics of Filipinos.

The first is *personalism*. This is described as the predominance of the subject over the object. It is not so much what a person does that matters but who he is; not what a person knows but whom he knows and who knows him; not so much on the objective reality of things but on the way such reality is understood. The hot button is not pressed unless a man's subjective core of self-worth is somehow touched. *

This explains why appeals for action among Filipinos are likely to fall on deaf ears unless the people concerned feel involved personally and not objectively. A printed invitation to a wedding, for example, is not very much effective unless it is preceded by a personal invitation from the host. This also accounts for the Filipino's being annoyed by a person who treats him like a servant, by rich people who refuse to talk to others, by people who intrude into conversations and by brutally frank persons.

Hence, among Filipinos it is important that one should be careful not to offend another person. Appeals should be made or presented subjectively, not objectively or at a distance and at best be made personally. Some practices that have developed from personalism are: (a) the practice of "bargaining" or *tawad* before closing a sale being preferred to the fixed price system of buying; (b) the *suki* system in which a buyer chooses a definite seller from whom she buys good regularly with discounts; this is preferred to shopping around for bargains all the time; (c) *utang na loob* which refers to a person's recognizing a debt of gratitude to one who has done him a big favor. This practice assumes an inviolable character depending on the person who gives the favor.

The second characteristic is *authoritarianism*. This refers to the high value placed on a person in authority—the boss or the expert. In their desire to remain safely on the approved side, Filipinos prefer to follow the dictates of those who are presumed to

73

know more than themselves. The Filipino clings to some power outside himself. This can be dependence upon tradition, social position, family name or some socially acknowledged authority, in order to reassure himself of his worth and of the righteousness of his acts.

A rather unusual example of this is the Filipino male's displaying the name of his tailor on a label outside the back pocket of his pants. This somehow gives him a feeling of belonging to the group who patronize the same tailor.

The Filipino of authoritarianism is not the stern, Germanic kind but a more paternalistic one. He expects his superior to be like a father to him and he depends upon people in authority. He is a very highly dependent person who values power. When a man is in power, he tries to get that man's favor; on the other hand, when he himself gets into power, he becomes very dominant. For the Filipino, to go against authority is a very big fault. He sets a high value on power and once he has power and authority, he holds on to it. This particular trait makes it so hard for him to delegate work. When he needs something, he will go all the way up and expect the top man to attend to him personally; if he does not get such attention, that man at the top is considered failing in his duty. He expects initiative to come from the top and those on top are supposed to plan everything out.

The third characteristic is *small-group centeredness*. Here the unit thought and actions within the nation is not so much of the individual, nor of the big group but of the small primary group. An individual finds his identity as part of the small group. He conforms to its attitudes, its moral and social norms. This is called "small-group thinking."

One's own small group to which a Filipino frequently applies the pronoun *kami* (meaning "we" excluding "you") places one's group at the moment in opposition to others. It is not the individual who decides; it is the small group to which he belongs that decides what to buy or what to wear.

It is this value that lies behind Filipinos' being annoyed by fellow Filipinos who speak in a foreign accent, servants who pretend to belong to high society, people in buses or jeepneys who talk loudly about themselves; or people of another religion who give out their own religious tracts.

Typical Filipino Traits

The Filipino has his own typical traits. A trait is a relatively persistent and consistent behavior pattern manifested in a wide range of circumstances. Some of the typical Filipino traits are discussed here:

1. *"Amor propio"* is a Spanish word which means self-love. It is a sense of self-esteem that prevents a person from swallowing his pride. It includes sensitivity to personal insult or affront. Amor propio, however, is not aroused by every insult, slight remark or offensive gesture. The stimulus that sets it off is only that which strikes at the Filipino's most highly valued attributes. An abandoned wife, for instance, will refuse to seek financial support from a husband who has abandoned her no matter how financially destitute she is. A son who has been disinherited will likewise refuse a reconciliation with his family even if the latter has expressed intentions of forgiving him. Amor propio is ego defensiveness, dignity or personal pride.

2. To a Filipino, *pakikisama* is a very important trait. This means the facility in getting along with others to maintain good and harmonious relationships in the home as well as outside the home. This leads to one's being socially accepted. One who has become successful in his field of endeavor has to be very careful about neglecting his friends lest they accuse him of becoming very proud and considering them no longer worthy of his friendship. In this respect, one of the best compliments that can be said of another is that he hasn't changed (*hindi nagbabago*). That is why there is so much backslapping and handshaking when Filipinos meet. Conversely, one of the worst things that can be said of a person is that he has changed a lot. He has forgotten how to get along well with others.

3. In spite of being a dependent person because of closeness to his family, the Filipino also has an innate desire to be on his own. *Pagsasarili* is the term which means that he has a burning desire to go it alone, to be a person in his own right. He may not say so in so many words; sometimes he is not even totally aware of this desire within him. But this is shown in his struggle to acquire a good education and improve his lot in life. Then with pride in earning a livelihood, he can be on his own without neglecting his family.

4. The Filipino is very sensitive to personal affront. He avoids feeling *hiya*, a painful emotion arising from a relationship with an authority figure or with society, inhibiting self-assertion in a situation which is perceived as dangerous to one's ego. It is a kind of anxiety, a fear of being left exposed, unprotected and unaccepted. It is a fear of abandonment, of "loss of soul," a loss not only of one's profession or even one's life but of something perceived as more valuable than life itself. Hiya is the value that regulates the Filipino's social behavior. When he violates a norm, the Filipino ordinarily feels a deep sense of shame, a realization of having failed to live up to the standards of society.

Just as one is very careful not to be subjected to embarrassment or *mapahiya* so does the Filipino make it a point not to cause another person to be embarrassed. In asking favors, for example, both parties are careful not to offend or appear offended. If a favor cannot be granted, it is the person who cannot oblige who apologizes for his failure to do so. He makes it clear that it is not because he does not want to give the favor but that other factors beyond his control keep him from doing so. So important to Filipinos is this trait that the saying goes: *"Hindi baleng huwag mo akong mahalin, huwag mo lang akong hiyain."* This means, "It does not matter if you don't love me as long as you don't shame me."

5. Most Filipinos are euphemistic. Euphemism which is the art of stating an unpleasant truth, opinion or request in as pleasant a manner as possible has long been highly prized in Philippine society and is no less highly regarded today. Harsh and insulting words are correspondingly devalued. Hence, it is not uncommon to hear the Filipino agree weakly instead of giving a flat refusal. "Maybe," "perhaps" or "I'll try" are his usual answers to questions to which a Westerner would readily say "no." This trait is related to his desire to please and not to offend someone.

6. Filipinos are generally a clean people. Every Filipino child is trained from his early years to keep his person clean. At home and in school, children are taught the need for maintaining cleanliness all the time.

Girls are trained early to do household work making them capable of keeping house when parents are away. Their mothers teach them diligently about personal hygiene regarding menstruation. It is quite noticeable how even among the poorer sections of cities, in the slums and in squatter areas, taking a bath is a daily ritual. Lack of private homes with bathrooms have not kept dwellers from bathing themselves even if they have to do it right along the streets in front of their houses.

The Filipinos always maintain cleanliness at home and their surroundings. However, they have the tendency to disregard cleanliness rules once they go to public places like parks and theaters.

Reciprocity as an Operating Principle

In the interdependent Philippine society, interpersonal relations revolve to a large extent around the granting and receiving of favors. A formalized pattern of behavior—reciprocity—has developed around this phase of interpersonal relations in order to keep them "smooth."

Reciprocity is defined as that principle of behavior wherein every service received, solicited or not, demands a return determined by the relative statuses of the parties involved and the kind of exchange at issue. There are three classifications of reciprocity: contractual, quasi-contractual and "utang na loob."

1. *Contractual reciprocity.* This supposes a voluntary agreement between two or more persons to behave toward one another in a specified way for a specified time in the future. The reciprocity arrangements (amount and form) are established beforehand. The participant knows what is expected of him and what he may expect of others. For example, upon completion of the work, the workmen are paid the agreed amount and the reciprocal relationship is then terminated. There is a minimum of effective sentiment or emotion in this kind of relationship.

2. *Quasi-contractual reciprocity.* The terms of repayment in this kind of relationship are not explicitly stated. Rather, they are implicit in the situation calling for these terms. Reciprocity is automatic without any specific prior arrangement. An example may be seen in the practice of *abuloy*. When someone dies, members of the community contribute money to the bereaved family who record these donations (abuloy). Reciprocal abuloy is given when someone in the donor's family dies. It is equivalent to the amount donated by the donor previously so neither party is

77

expected to feel grateful.

3. *Utang-na-loob* is an ancient Filipino operating principle. It is the reciprocity generated when a transfer of goods or services takes place between individuals belonging to two different groups. Since one does not ordinarily expect favors from anyone not of his own group, a service of this kind throws the norm into bold relief. Furthermore, it compels the recipient to show his gratitude properly by returning the favor with interest to be sure that he does not remain in the other person's debt. A common Tagalog saying which shows that gratitude is highly valued in the Philippine society runs thus, *"Ang hindi marunong lumingon sa pinanggalingan, hindi makararating sa paroroonan* (He who does not look back to the place he has been to will not get to where he is going)."

The degree of debt of gratitude depends to a large extent on the favor received. For instance, a sick child may be cured by a doctor who does not think it right to send a bill. Or even if he does, the fact that he has saved the child makes the parents forever indebted to the doctor.

A child is indebted to his parents for his life and is considered ungrateful, "walang utang na loob" if he fails to provide for them in their old age.

The Filipino usually feels "shamed" *napapahiya* if his token of gratitude is not received. It makes him feel that his gift is not good enough. Or he interprets it as a sign that the other party wants to end their relationship. No one would probably dare ask for another favor if his token of appreciation is not accepted. It would mean that he would forever be in the other person's debt—*nakalubog na sa utang*—"deep in debt." Or it can be interpreted that the person who continues to ask for favors can't take the cue that the other party doesn't want to grant him future favors. Such person is *walang pakiramdam* (literally "no feeling" i.e., callous) or *makapal ang mukha* ("thick faced," i.e., shameless).

The Filipino cannot run his office as impersonally as the Westerner. In many offices, one usually gets the impression that when he gets his papers processed, for example, a favor has been done for him. It is not unusual, therefore, for people who have received such "favors" to feel that they should offer a "reward." These rewards may take the form of, say, fruits and vegetables, eggs, a sack of rice, etc. and are given at a "decent" time, i.e., not too soon after the favor has been received. Giving money as a payment for a favor, however, is usually considered insulting.

Where a Westerner would simply write a "thank you" note for a favor received and consider his "debt" paid, the Filipino does not write such a note but considers himself indebted and waits for a chance to return the favor.

Furthermore, debts of gratitude, big or small, cannot really be paid at all, as shown in another Tagalog saying: "*Ang utang na loob, napakaliit man, utang at utang din kahit mabayaran. Sa pakitang loob at tapat na damay ay walang sukat maitimbang* (A favor, no matter how small, is a debt we must never forget since no money can ever fully repay it)."

Respect for the Dead

Filipinos pay much respect to their dead. They believe in life after death and they have lengthy and colorful funeral ceremonies and rituals; wakes or vigils for the dead last three, five or seven days. Notice of death of a loved one is spread to relatives and friends by word of mouth or through obituaries. They are expected to condole with the members of the family of the dead, to give monetary contributions in condolence and keep vigil until the burial day.

Calling at the Funeral Home

Usually the body of the deceased remains at the funeral home until the day of interment. Often the family receives close friends and relatives there, rather than at home. People who wish to pay their respects but are not close to the bereaved may stop in and sign the registry book that is always provided by the funeral parlor. Their signatures are formal, including their titles and addresses.

When one does not personally know the deceased, but only his close relatives, flowers may be sent to them, with a card addressed to one of the family on which is written "with sympathy," with deepest sympathy," or, if appropriate, "with love and sympathy."

Vigil in the Home

In the provinces and in some cases also in cities, families keep vigil for their dead in their own homes. This is more private than in funeral homes and expenses are less. Relatives and friends stay overnight until the time of burial. Meanwhile the family also give food and refreshments to those who come to sympathize with them.

The Funeral Service

Before interment, the body of the dead is brought to the church where final rites are held. In the Catholic church the ceremony may include the celebration of the Holy Mass or it may not. In Protestant churches services are held with singing of hymns and prayers and rituals read by the ministers.

All members of the family of the deceased and close friends are expected to attend the funeral. After church rites, they all follow the funeral procession to the grave site where they stay until the body is interred.

Mourning Practices

It is a common practice for a widow go wear all-black attire for one year. A woman who has lost a grown-up daughter or son may wear black for a year or at least six months. Men go into mourning by wearing a simple black pin on their shirts.

Presently, however, more and more people wear dark blue, brown, white or other inconspicuous colors instead of all-black dresses when in mourning.

After interment Catholics hold nightly prayers at home for the dead for nine days. On the ninth night, the bereaved family invite all relatives and friends to a sumptuous meal in celebration of the end of the novena.

Weddings, birthday celebrations and other social activities in the family are not celebrated with elaborate or pompous festivities within a year after the death of a family member. In some particular places, the widow cannot attend any social function for a year.

All Saints Day

November 1st is a national holiday in the Philippines. It is a day set aside for honoring and remembering the dead and keeping vigil at the cemeteries. Lighted candles and beautiful flowers adorn the cleaned and polished graves as relatives pay homage to the departed.

Children and pranksters spend Halloween night snatching chickens and other belongings from yards and porches. These items are later ransomed for coins or a bowl of hot *ginatan*, a native delicacy. *Undasan*, a Filipino version of "trick or treat" is very much a part of Halloween celebration.

7 SEX, COURTSHIP AND MARRIAGE IN THE PHILIPPINES

Filipino Sexual Values

The *culture of insecurity* that the Philippines has lived through for centuries, has in an indirect way affected the Filipino's sexual values. For the centuries of uncertainty and insecurity have made the Filipino realize that the only security he can find available to him is the security offered *within* and by his family.

In order to further enhance the welfare of his family, the Filipino strives to enlarge the power of his family through the pro-creation of many children since, in a rural setting, more children would definitely mean more hands to till the land, more hands to harvest the yield, more hands to do house chores, and more arms to protect the family in case of attack. This is one reason why Western propagandists on family planning have not been totally accepted by Filipinos.

Based on this premise, masculinity in the Philippines is equaled with the man's ability to procreate children and femininity, in turn, is equated with a woman's capacity to bear them. A young man is usually asked in his early teens if he was already *nabinyagan* (literally, *baptized;* idiomatically, *initiated into sexual relations*) and he is then teased because "he is not yet a man" since he has not yet been so initiated. Newly-wed Filipino males are also teased that they might already be *pundido* (literally, *put-off;* idiomatically, *impotent*) if their wives have not conceived a few months after marriage.

The woman is considered a full woman if she is able to bear

a child. The woman who conceives soon after marriage is the object not only of the husband's attention and compassion but of all the relatives, especially the family of the groom. On the other hand, a bride who does not conceive after a reasonable period of time is often teased that she would be returned to her parents.

"Machismo"

The tendency of the Filipino to equate masculinity or virility with the ability to procreate is also at the root of some Filipino male's irresponsibility and infidelity that occurs after marriage. Since a man is more of a man if he is able to have a woman and to beget children, his "extra-curricular activities" are regarded as part of his *pagkalalake* (being a man).

One speaks of "machismo"—possibly meaning "manhood" but more accurately indicating the man's cultural manifestation of his virility. Through sexual relations he can prove his capability, while otherwise he has few possibilities of exercising his "prowess." The Filipino father exercises this type of authority in his family, resulting in a state of submission by the woman and her daughters, while fostering in the male descendants a feeling of superiority.

Unlike the man, the Filipino woman is considered a *true woman* only if she bears children and is "close to God, is hardworking, is faithful and remains loyal to those dear to her." Before marriage, the Filipino woman is expected to keep herself a virgin for the man she will marry. Unwed men are not expected to do so; he is in fact given unlimited freedom in sexual matters as part of his pagkalalake. This is why Filipino girls must be watched and chaperoned; they are to be protected from the fact that boys are privileged to do as they please! Incidentally, when a man has many daughters and no sons or fewer sons than daughters, people say that his daughters are his *pambayad ng utang ng kanyang pagkalalake* (payment for his debts for being a man). In short, daughters are regarded as a Filipino male's punishments for his sexual irresponsibilities before or during his marriage: it is his turn to protect his daughters from the sexual irresponsibilities of other men.

If the Filipino woman is expected to keep herself a virgin for the man she will later on marry, she is expected to remain loyal to the same man whom she married no matter what happens. Even if her husband proves to be unfaithful, she is expected to bear this as part of his male weakness (*kahinaan ng isang lalake*) and as part of the painful experiences of married life.

A Filipina is not as openly provocative, and sexually aggressive as her Western counterpart. The Filipino culture, inspite of some minorities' ultra progressiveness still considers as the ideal image of a woman one who is shy, demure, modest, self-effacing, and loyal to the end.

Taboos on Premarital Relationship

In the Philippines free love and premarital sexual relationship is not recognized and accepted. Society imposes strong pressures against premarital sexual relations. This pressure may be attributed to the strong influence of Christianity. Furthermore the reasons for the existence of the *taboo* are the following:[21]

1. There is the ever-present and inescapable danger of the girl's becoming pregnant.
2. There is the probability of catching venereal disease.
3. The girl may acquire a bad reputation.
4. Sex is likely tc be cheapened in the eyes of the two persons.
5. There is often little opportunity for adequate sexual education on the part of the girl and the boy.

Generally, Filipino parents are opposed to premarital sexual relationship even during the period of engagement. However, due to the growing independence of young Filipinos from the mores of their parents, intimacies in the relationship between young men and young women are covertly practiced even before the altar date. There was a time in the history of the Filipinos when a simple kiss was interpreted to mean a proposal for marriage. Today, in the urban and rural areas of the country, kissing has become an ordinary practice.

The Double Standard

In the Filipino value orientation, a man is brought up with the orientation of strength, boldness and aggression. He is allowed more freedom of action than a woman simply because of the usually ascribed adult traits distinctive of the male—responsibility, independence and conviction. Oftentimes, these traits are shown under the guise of masculinity—that is, in terms of muscles, sexual prowess, booze, cigarettes. The Filipino male is to drink, smoke and have as many women as their energy will allow them prior to and after marriage. A man who is promiscuous is considered simply as demonstrating his pagkalalake (manliness). A woman who is promiscuous, however, is considered *masamang babae* (bad woman). The young Filipino male from his teens on is free generally to come and go as he pleases with little or without direct supervision by his parents. "Boys are boys" is the accepted dictum. However, the young Filipino girl is carefully supervised in her social activities until the time of her marriage.

The manifestation of sexual behavior in the Philippines is best illustrated through a long-held tradition of initiation commensurate to rites de passage, a phrase coined by anthropologist Arnold van Gennep. This rite known as *binyag* (baptism) has come to be generally viewed as a positive means of affirming manhood and maleness. It necessitates every boy and young man to go through two stages to become a complete man.

The first phase is *tuli* (circumcision), which, at present, is still considered the flagship and test of manhood. Circumcision carries very much weight upon the behavior of an uncircumcised —he becomes the object of a fair game for a lot of needling, taunting and ribbing from both circumcised friends and enemies. The Filipino boys usually undergo circumcision upon reaching the age between eight and ten. Those in the urban communities have their operations in the hospital, where many boys are circumcised as soon as they are born. Those who undergo the traditional operation do so voluntarily. In both rural and urban communities there are a number of specialists who perform the operation. Most operations are done on Holy Saturday of the Lenten season, but they can also be done anytime. The preference for the Holy Week is the belief that "bleeding is not profuse during this season." The place of operation is usually in a tree-covered backyard in the rural communities, or in an isolated *barong-barong* (shanty) in the urban center.

Phase two is the first sexual intercourse or the so-called binyag. This may be alluded to as pre-marital defloration in the case of a female. Because of the still prevalently high premium put on would-be virgin brides, the first attempt is, most of the time done with a prostitute. This means that now the boy is a man and he should be introduced to manly things. Members of his peer group accompany him; sometimes, they pay for the "encounter." Sexual intercourse is not a precondition to becoming a man in the rural area. Circumcised boys nevertheless are considered clean and, many young people believe, they are much preferred by women than those who are not circumcised. The latter are known as *supot*, and they are not considered men yet. One is called a sissy. In some cases where there are no prostitutes, a *bakla* (homosexual) is invited to binyag or initiate sexually the neophyte.

A male sexual behavior associated with adolescence is the *gapang* or sleep crawling. In both rural and urban communities this takes place. Gapang is a practice young males resort to in order to experience sexual intercourse with a girl he likes. Although this appears by all means to be one form of rape, Filipinos do not recognize the act as such. The term for rape is *paggahasa*. Gapang involves "crawling beside a girl at night when most of the older household members are asleep or are not at home." Usually there is a previous understanding between the boy and the girl that the gapang will take place. This happens or is deliberately done when the girl's parents strongly object to her choice and put up barriers to discourage the affair. Should it be known that the girl has lost her virginity to her boyfriend, marriage is the only way to rectify the damage and restore the status of the family before the eyes of the community.

Gapang is sometimes resorted to in order to overcome unrequited love. It becomes a mechanism to maintain the image of the offender in the community which is threatened by his being a rejected lover. It likewise reinforces the man's acceptance of certain locally unconventional sexual escapades. Because gapang is also used by the male to "even up with the girl who rejects him," the technique restores his image and strengthens his pagkalalake. This then takes the form of *rape* since it is without the girl's consent.

The Querida System

What divorce is to the Westerners, *querida system* is to a few Filipino males. This is a way of life wherein a married man maintains a mistress, sometimes to the extent of including a second home. The Filipino married male who keeps a *querida* provides the mistress subsistence and goes home to her once in a while but he is ever careful to keep the relationship a secret from his lawful wife. If his mistress bears him a child, he usually supports the bastard but is very careful not to acknowledge the child's paternity. This is not only because his wife might discover it but also because he might be accused of immorality especially if he is a government official or employee with civil service eligibility. This behavior is generally considered "normal" since it goes along with the concept of "machismo." The "machismo" complex somehow encourages the Filipino male to take on a sexual role which could only be verified by the peer group to which he belongs in terms of the number of affairs he maintains and children he sires either with his legitimate wife or his mistresses. In fact, it is not surprising to find a laborer or jeepney driver earning hardly P300 a month, to have two or three *kabits* (mistresses).

For the mistress, having a child means a sure source of income. A man may not support his mistress but he can be coerced into supporting the child. Since being a mistress is a temporary affair wherein youth is dissipated in the process, without a child, she gets into a pitiful situation in old age.

Philandering by the Filipino male is not very much looked down upon in the Filipino culture. Because he is a man, he can be forgiven for taking too much sexual freedom. He just wants to prove his masculinity. On the other hand, Filipino wives feel that sex is primarily the husband's pleasure, so it can be denied him if he misbehaves. "Outside the *kulambo*" (mosquito net) is a punishment meted out to a husband who has been caught by his wife having an affair with another woman.

The Child

In the Philippines, children are much desired and enjoyed. In the rural areas, it is common to hear babies cry, quarrels between husbands and wives about the baby's welfare, voices of mothers, female siblings or even fathers rocking babies to sleep. In the cities, adults cuddling a child early in the morning or late in the afternoon is a familiar street corner scene. Both males and females take part in the care of babies. Children are fondled whenever possible. A child for the Filipino parents and adults is said to be a source of joy. Furthermore, a child is viewed as a source of strength and relief during critical moments.

When children are extremely naughty, the rod is not spared. Filipinos agree that children are children and must be disciplined while young. However, most Filipino parents are quite permissive with children and punish them only as a last recourse. A child is considered a gift from God, the grace derived from divine blessings, the result of clean, honest living. It is believed that parents who do not welcome the arrival of a child or who deprive those who are born with the necessary adult attention and care are punished—they either suffer from a lingering illness or from a hard economic life.

The child is considered as an evidence of love. Children are viewed as the cementing element in the relationship between husbands and wives. It is also believed that the sex of children must be evenly distributed. If the couple has children of the same sex—i.e., all boys or all girls—child-bearing is not complete; the family is not balanced. Thus pregnancy continues until a child of the opposite sex is born. In many cases, adoption is resorted to when children of the same sex continue to come. The concept of balance in sex number of children is closely associated with the concept of *buenas* or good fortune.

Children are considered as investments. It is believed that by having more children, an individual has more chances that one of them will succeed in the future; hence, a better economic and social status. For the Filipino, children are necessary in order to maintain the family line. Until a boy is born to a couple they must not stop bearing children.

Courtship and Mate Selection

It is frequently said that in the Philippines a boy courts the mother as well as the daughter. Among the Tagalogs, there is a period of courting, called *nanlulusong*, in which the boy works with the parents of the girl so that the parents can observe the

88

boy's real character. If the boy is unacceptable to the parents, the courtship is generally terminated. Because it is a familial alliance, the parents' opinions are "like the word of God." Religion is employed to reinforce the will of the parents. A couple disobeying their parents and eloping, for example, would not enjoy the "graces of God." Barrenness is often explained as a "parental curse," the couple having ignored the decisions of their parents.

A man sets out to gather and chop wood, fetch water and till the woman's father's farm, if only to win her heart and her family's regard. This is, in fact, the code of courtship among the Tagalogs; proving that, even in love, industry and patience have their reward. Among the island people of Mindoro and the Visayas, *harana* (serenade) or songs make the most romantic expressions of love. Moonlit meadows provide the ever-romantic setting. The young man, accompanying himself with a guitar, unburdens his feelings in a song. The girl, wakened by his serenade, responds with a song, too, And the singing goes on till they reach an understanding. Another practice is the *tuksuhan* (teasing). Romance, too, blooms with playful proddings and stolen glances. Intermittent with easy laughters and gentle teasings, love is hinted—not by the admirer himself but by his friends and hers. The girl welcomes all this, if she secretly favors him. But he must be quick to get her hints and see beneath her coyness and feigned disinterest so he can express his love, confidently, on his own. In the *pamamanhikan*, when the man, so to speak, "asks for the woman's hand," the last and crucial step in the courtship, the elders are brought together and they, in a language so indirect and derived from traditions, manage to settle details of the marriage of their young.

Courtship among ancient Filipinos revolved around the dowry. The "dowry" was a gift turned over by the groom to the bride's parent practically in exchange for his bride. The terms of a dowry were discussed with great tact and diplomacy by elderly representatives of both parties. It was customary for the wise parent to turn over the dowry to her daughter as part of her paraphernal property brought into the marriage; but, if it was kept by the parents it was returned to the groom in case of separation. The disposition of the dowry as decided upon by the elders reveals who is to blame for the failure of the marriage. The wife keeps it if her husband is to blame.

This system of preparing the dowry for the bride still has its vestiges in the wedding customs of the Philippines. Unlike the Western and some Asian wedding customs, in Filipino weddings, the bridegroom assumes all the responsibilities for the preparations including the wedding dress and the celebration. This contrasts with the practice in Western societies where this type of expense is cared for by the parents of the bride. In western areas, some brides would feel socially disgraced to have the groom assume any wedding expense except the purchase of the marriage license and the fee of the clergyman or the judge who officiates at the ceremony; in the Philippines, some brides would be shocked at the suggestion that they share in the cost of the wedding.

In many rural areas, indirect courtship with gifts for the bride's family and negotiations by intermediaries is still popular. Sometimes, the young swain may approach the barrio captain who in turn will approach the parents and arrange for a meeting between the parents of the young man and the parents of his potential bride. If the grandparents are living they must be consulted. Marriage is an alliance of families and not individuals, and before the final approval can be given all the relatives have a chance to voice out their feelings.

The individualistic trend of the gesellschaft society has begun to manifest itself in urban areas. Here, the family influence is still important, but the young Filipinos are given a greater chance to manifest their own choice. In some circles the chaperon has been replaced by group dating on the theory that this is less burdensome on the parents, and the presence of a group will prevent infractions of the mores concerning pre-marital behavior. This is the so-called "barkada system." In still other circles, engaged couples may be allowed to go to social affairs without being a member of the group or under the eye of a chaperon, but this is still regarded in many groups as a rather questionable practice. Free association of the young is thought to threaten both the concept of pre-marital chastity and the influence of the family over the marital choice.

In Filipino society, the chastity of the bride is regarded as the greatest virtue, and the individual romantic impulses are considered less important than the judgment of the family group on the suitability of the marriage partner. Concern over chastity goes beyond the limits of technical virginity (that is, the breaking of the hymen) and it is often thought that any kind of association with the opposite sex beyond the most forward type makes the bride less desirable to the future husband. This situation is moderated somewhat in the *damay* (gemeinschaft) setting of the rural society in which girls are heavily chaperoned but may associate with a large circle of men inside the family group.

Dating

Courtship, as a process, involves several stages. The first stage is dating. Dating, from the point of view of the Filipinos, is one way of exploring or getting to know each other's personality. The Filipino concept of dating has some similarities with that of the western idea of dating. Westerners usually consider dating as an end in itself, showing no further emotional involvement; it provides an opportunity for friendly relationship with the opposite sex and serves as the basis for the selection of a partner.

Although Filipinos are greatly influenced by Western concepts, there are still some slight variations regarding their concept of dating. Today, from the time a man and a woman start dating, it is presumed there is already a slight degree of emotional involvement between the two. Dating in the Western culture is done with little or no parental supervision at all. Among Filipinos getting to know each other with little or no parental supervision at all is done in group activities such as going on outings and attending socials. It is here where they are provided an opportunity for friendly relations with the opposite sex. The moment they go dating, parents' guidance and assistance are usually asked, since there is already an emotional attachment between the two. While Western women would not mind being dated by several men, Filipino women don't give much value to dating a lot of men in the sense that they are afraid that they might be called or branded as "easy-going," "cheap," and a "woman of low reputation." In the Philippines, the moment a woman goes out with a man, it is presumed that they have started to go steady. Dating several men in order to select the best marriage partner is looked down upon by Filipinos.

Among Filipinos the stage of private understanding in courtship usually takes place during the period of going steady where a man openly declares his love for the woman and his desire to marry her. Here a Westerner would be surprised to receive no immediate response from the Filipino woman. Convention in the Philippines dictates that the woman should not give at once any verbal response, whether positive or negative. In spite of the man's knowledge of custom, the Filipino male insists in getting a response with no expectation of getting any. Among the Filipino males the technique is to invite the girl for a date after the declaration. Should she accept his invitation after his having spoken of his love and affection for her, it is considered a clear indication that the woman has accepted his proposal. Such relationship is usually kept secret by the two participants.

Whatever plans engaged Filipinos make are still subject to the approval of the parents of both. They also have to follow the ritual set by culture. If during the engagement period premarital relations result in pregnancy, Philippine culture dictates that she must, by all means, run after the man so that the engagement may materialize into marriage. On the other hand, culture dictates that the engaged woman must take a philosophical attitude toward a broken engagement, for after all she might have escaped an unhappy marriage for the rest of her life.

Marriage

In the Philippines, marriage is viewed as a permanent contract, an "inviolable social institution" (Civil Code No. 14). There is no divorce in the Philippines except among the Muslims and indigenous religious groups. Legal separation involves separation from bed and board but does not allow a second marriage while the first spouse is still alive. Because of the legal complications involved in a formal court separation and the stigma which can be brought upon the families and the children in proving adultery or concubinage on the part of a parent, legal separation is not too common. However, separation without the court sanction (called *hiwalay*) is not uncommon in the cities and even in the rural areas. The spouse may form another companionship marriage. The Filipino term for this type of alliance is *kinakasama*.

Most families stay together regardless of how the husband and wife feel about each other due to the cultural and religious forces which pull them together. The first social pressure derives from the system of *marriage arrangement*. In many Philippine rural areas, marriage follows a group decision by the parents and relatives of the bride and groom. Unlike in the Western culture, marriage is seen not so much as the joining in matrimony of a devoted and love-struck boy and girl; rather it is an inter-family alliance deliberately entered into for sound economic or other reasons. The alliance is symbolized by the union of a representative couple and sealed by the birth of their first child.

Before the wedding is celebrated, a number of practices serve to involve more and more relatives in the event which is to occur. In some Philippine provinces, it is the girl's father or mother who decides whether a daughter may be given away in marriage to a suitor who has passed the test. When this time comes, the girl's parents ask the young man to inform his parents of their desire to talk with them. A certain date is set aside for the purpose. The suitor's parents, together with their kin and friends arrive at the bride's home, bringing with them food and drinks. It is during this occasion that the girl's parents state the conditions and demands the accomplishments upon which lies the consummation of the wedding. This event is known as the *bulungan* (whispering session). The dowry usually varies. Some parents ask for land, for money, or a house or work animals, or all of them. All expenses to be incurred during the wedding party must be shouldered by the bridegroom's parents. Several hogs, chickens and cattle should be butchered to feed every invited and uninvited visitor who will surely attend the party. After the wedding party that usually lasts for two days, the newly-married woman goes with her parents-in-law while the husband is left in his father-in-law's house. Only after four or nine days does the husband go to see and sleep for the first time with his lawful wife.

Relatives of both sides are interested in seeing that the couple, once married, should stay married. Aside from obtaining the consent of each and every relative, contribution follows, especially on the boy's side. Both parties being so involved would see to it that such a family alliance for which they voted and even spent is forever kept intact.

The practice of Filipino newlyweds living near relatives adds another social pressure favoring the stability of the union called *marriage surveillance*. Relatives are not only interested in the duration of the marriage they planned; they are on hand to make sure it works. The eyes and ears and tongues of relatives are effective tools in stopping man and wife from doing things locally considered bad for the marriage. An economic pressure that keeps man, wife and children together is the formation of the family as a *functional economic unit.* In most rural families in the Philippines each member of the family has its own special work-role, and the family that works together has good reason for staying together. A very strong factor in preserving the Filipino family group is the *conjugal bond,* that is the legal and sacramental contract joining husband and wife and the internal sense of obligation and privilege existing in the mind and heart of each spouse.

The Wedding

Marriages take many forms in the Philippines: a church wedding in white for Christians; a civil ceremony or "registry marriage" by a judge, mayor, or minister and the new phenomenon of "mass weddings" on special occasions.22

Males above twenty but under twenty-five years of age, or females above eighteen but under twenty-three years of age, are obliged to ask their parents' or guardians' consent to the intended marriage. If they do not obtain such consent, the marriage shall not take place till after three months following the completion of the publication of the application for marriage license. A sworn statement by the contracting parties to the effect that such consent is given shall accompany the application for marriage license. Should the parents or guardian refuse to give any consent, this fact shall be stated in the sworn declaration (New Civil Code of the Philippines Article 62).

The contracting parties must first file an application for a marriage license with the office of the Civil Registrar in any municipality or chartered city. Two forms must be dully accomplished, one by the groom-to-be and the other by the bride-to-be. While this form should be filed in the municipality where either the man or the woman resides, convention dictates that the form be filed in the municipality of the woman. The applicants are then asked to wait for ten days for the license to be issued. During this period, the applicants' names are posted at the bulletin board of the Civil Registrar's Office. The ten-day waiting period

94

allows time for the parties to think over the seriousness of marriage. If there are impediments to the marriage, the public posting is supposed to enable those concerned to voice their objections.

Although a civil marriage performed by a justice of the peace is legitimate, most brides and grooms in the Philippines prefer a church wedding. The preparations called for in this kind of a wedding are the following:[23]

1. *Wedding announcements.* The wedding announcement is formally made by the parents of the bride or her guardian.

2. *Despedida de soltera.* This term can be literally translated into "goodbye to spinsterhood." It is a party given for the bride-to-be by her friends, the equivalent of the "shower" explained below.

Before the wedding day, the bride-to-be attends to the preparation of her trousseau and hope chest. She is usually the recipient of good wishes, showers, and parties. The groom, on the other hand, may be occupied in looking for a house where the couple will stay after marriage.

3. *The shower.* This is a party given in honor of the bride-to-be by her girl friends. Here, she is given appropriate gifts, often things she would need to start housekeeping with. Traditionally, this serves as an instrument for imparting to her some knowledge about marriage, but today the real motive is usually overlooked and the party becomes an event for teasing the bride-to-be.

4. *Date and Time of the wedding.* More often than not, parents have a direct say in the setting of the date, and in this particular aspect of preparation certain superstitious beliefs are often taken into serious consideration. For example, the marriage should take place on a day before the full moon; a day when the moon is waning in considered unlucky. However, nowadays, the whole matter is left to the couple, specially if the parents of both participants are college-educated. When the date of the wedding is set, the time and place will likewise be agreed upon.

5. *The wedding ensemble.* Generally, the preparation of the wedding ensemble is left entirely in the hands of the bride-to-be. Custom dictates, however, that the man or the man's parents shoulder the expenses. On the other hand, there are times when the bride-to-be or her parents take care of this matter, specially if they are relatively well-to-do.

6. *The wedding invitation.* Invitations to the wedding are prepared early enough. The correct form for a wedding invitation can be seen at the printer's office. All that is needed is to supply him with the proper names as well as the date, the time and the place of both the wedding ceremony and the reception. Invitations are sent out early enough to reach those invited on time. The list of guests is made out by both parties, usually with the help of parents.

7. *Wedding rehearsals.* In the Philippines a wedding rehearsal is an exception rather than the rule. The families and friends of the bride or groom do not worry about seating arrangements in the church. It is enough that they attend the wedding. Those who participate in the ceremony rely upon a church assistant, usually the *sacristian mayor*, to instruct them on what to do. However, at present a well organized church's priest or pastor sometimes requires the bride and groom not only to attend a seminar on marriage but also to rehearse the wedding ceremony together with the whole entourage one or two days before the wedding day.

8. *The wedding reception.* The setting for the wedding reception usually depends upon the place where the wedding ceremony will take place. Traditionally, wedding receptions are held at the home of the bride, and they become the affair of the entire community, not of a selected few only. Thus, the wedding reception becomes a heavy financial burden on the groom and his parents. Today the trend is to have the wedding ceremony in the city and the reception at a restaurant.

9. *The wedding trip.* Having a wedding trip immediately after the wedding ceremony and reception is a practice introduced by the Westerners in the Philippines. Among urban Filipinos the wedding trip, sometimes called "honeymoon" is going to Baguio or to Tagaytay City. Among the more affluent ones, it means a trip to United States, Hawaii, Singapore or Hong Kong. Among the rural folks such wedding trip is not so much practiced. The newlyweds start building their own home instead.

The Wedding Day

Before the wedding ceremony, the bridesmaids meet at the house of the bride, where they receive their bouquets. When everyone is ready, the bride's mother drives away to the church in the first car, with perhaps others of her children or one of the bridesmaids with her. Maid of honor, bridesmaids and flower girls follow. Last of all, the bride and her father. This car remains in front of the church entrance.

Meanwhile, about an hour before the ceremony, the ushers arrive at the church. Their boutonnieres, sent by the groom, are waiting in the vestibule. The ushers most likely to recognize the friends and members of each family are detailed to the center aisle. Those who will escort the mothers of the bride and groom are assigned.

A few pews on either side of the center aisle are reserved for the immediate families of the couple. The left is the "bride's side" and the right the groom's.

As the wedding music is played, the bridal procession starts usually in this order: (1) the ushers coming in by twos, (2) the veil, candle, and cord sponsors coming in by pairs, (3) the bridegroom flanked by his parents, (4) the bride's mother escorted by an usher, (5) the principal sponsors in pairs, (6) the ring bearer, (7) the flower girl who throws flowers as she walks in (8) the bridesmaids and the maid or matron of honor walking singly, and finally, the bride at her father's left walking more slowly than the others before them.

At the chancel, the ushers stand one at the right and another at the left. The bridesmaids stand at the left, with the maid of honor standing opposite the best man at the right side. The flower girl stands in front of the bridesmaids; the ring bearer in front of the best man. The bridegroom stands at the right with the best man beside him. The principal sponsors are seated, the ladies at the left side and the gentlemen at the right near the bride's and the bridegroom's parents.

As soon as the priest comes in to officiate in the ceremony, the bride takes the bridegroom's left arm and they go slowly up the altar. The best man follows to the right of the groom while the maid of honor follows at the left of the bride. The bridal bouquet is handed over to the maid of honor.

In Roman Catholic ceremonies, the bride's father joins his wife as soon as the bridegroom takes his daughter's hand. In Protestant weddings, the father remains at his daughter's left until he is called upon by the minister to give away her hand in marriage. Then he sits beside his wife.

97

Catholic ceremonies usually are held with the Nuptial mass as its high point. Here the members of the bridal party as well as the other Catholic members take part in the Holy Communion.

Wedding fees paid to the church differ in amount depending upon the kind of ceremony desired by the couple to be married. More simple weddings cost less while those with all the trimmings —flowers, lights, soloists, organist, carpets, etc. call for bigger fees that may run up to thousands of pesos.

The Wedding Reception

After the wedding ceremony, the priest declares the couple husband and wife and then a recessional follows with the couple going out first. The other participants follow in the reverse order than they came in. The bridal party and all the other guests then go to the reception place which in the city may be in a plush restaurant or an eatery or at the bride's house in the rural places.

Gifts to the newlyweds are brought to the reception or are sent to the bride's residence.

What to Wear to a Wedding

Weddings are usually formal affairs so guests dress formally: a long skirt or formal dress for the women, and coat and tie or "barong tagalog" for the men. Black is never worn in wedding feasts. Black for Filipinos is a symbol of sorrow. Short dresses or pantsuits for the women and sport shirts for men are not worn in wedding ceremonies, either.

Women should wear modest clothes; no revealing, plunging necklines or backless, strapless gowns. A long skirt, or one that covers the knees and a long-sleeved blouse is in good taste. They also put on their jewelry. Children wear their party clothes.

8 FILIPINO PRACTICES ON VARIOUS OCCASIONS

A foreigner who stays in the Philippines—whether in cities like Manila or Cebu or in rural places like towns and barrios—is likely to note some peculiar customs and practices of Filipinos on various occasions. This chapter explains some of those practices so that the expatriate can understand better how to behave and relate to the people around him.

Taking Public Conveyances

A great number of Filipinos take public conveyances like jeepneys, buses, tricycles, carretelas, in going places—to offices, schools, markets, etc. Only a privileged few own cars. Hence, the following are worth noting when taking a public vehicle:

1. The jeepney is the most common public conveyance that brings people to places at a minimum cost of ninety centavos in the city and one peso or more in the provinces. Being a music lover, the typical jeepney driver must have his music, hence the prevalence of stereophonic wonders in buses and jeeps—radios, tape discs, amplifiers—all supposed to entertain the riding public. Some drivers, not content with just music put in strobelights, psychedelic posters and other contraptions, the more the merrier, making his vehicle not only a jukebox on wheels but a fair as well.

Passengers meet the jeep or bus at its nearest and most accessible stopping place to be assured of a seat.

When alighting, the passenger shouts aloud, *Para*!! (stop) especially if there is loud music inside the vehicle. While some male commuters alight even when the vehicle is still in motion, it is always safer to wait until it gets to a complete stop.

In buses which are crowded especially during peak hours—seven to eight o'clock in the morning or five to seven in the evening—women now take rides even if they have to stand. A few gentlemen still offer their seats to women who in turn thank them for their generosity.

2. In crossing avenues and streets it is advisable to use pedestrian lanes whenever one is visible. Using street corners where traffic lights are placed is a safety precaution. Jaywalking or crossing a street carelessly is punishable in big cities so pedestrians are expected to cross at safe places to avoid being fined by the police.

3. In taking jeepney rides, passengers pay directly to the driver due to the absence of a conducter who charges fare. When seated at the farthest end from the driver, one passes on his fare through the other passengers who readily help in having the money get to the driver.

4. Boisterous laughing and talking aloud in jeeps and buses are looked down upon as rude behavior. It is preferable to remain quiet during the trip or talk only in subdued tones.

Taking a Taxi

Taxis abound in big towns and cities in the country. Each taxi has a taxi meter which the driver turns on as soon as the trip starts. While most drivers should know all places that the passengers need to go to, it is best to be able to guide the driver as to one's destination to avoid big expenses due to long, unnecessary trip distances. Some unscrupulous taxi drivers abuse their passengers by taking long, round-about trips if they feel that their passengers do not exactly know how to get to their destination.

In some cities taxis do not have meters but the drivers have fixed amounts charged for definite areas of destination. This is specified by law on public utility vehicles.

One who has no idea as to the correct amount to pay for a taxi ride should inquire from policemen or other authorities before getting into a bargain with a taxi driver. That way he won't be overcharged for his trip. This is applicable when taxis have no taxi meters due to one reason or another.

When an empty taxi passes by and one flags it down but the driver has his meter covered with a towel and he refuses to stop, it means that he is on his way to Car Barn or he is hurrying to take his meal. He won't take any passenger then.

If a passenger leaves something by mistake in a taxi he took, he can at once call up a popular radio station that gives out public service announcements. Taxi drivers usually have radios and they listen to these popular programs. Most of these drivers will be too willing and honest enough to return the lost belongings if the owner gives his address to the radio announcer.

Should a passenger encounter any problem with a taxi driver, he or she should take down the name and number of the taxi and report it to the nearest police station or to the Ministry of Tourism. Local authorities are very much concerned about tourists and foreigners being treated very well by drivers.

Driving in the Philippines

Driving cars in city streets and highways in the Philippines may not be as easy as it should be. Drivers' behavior often makes it necessary for the motorist to take extra precautions or to anticipate what the other driver might do in order to avoid getting into accidents. Here are some typical practices of Filipino drivers:[24]

1. A driver's license is obtained at a moderate fee required by the Land Transportation Commission yearly or every three years. It is also available in LTC offices in provincial capitals over the country.

2. In the Philippines all drivers "Drive Right." They always drive on the right hand lane of the road.

3. It is not unusual to see jeepney drivers in towns and cities who stop abruptly within the lane to load or unload passengers; sometimes they even fail to give any stop signal. Taxi drivers may suddenly halt in the middle of the road when a passenger flags them down. It is always good to maintain a safe following distance.

4. Many pedestrians prefer to walk on the road rather than on sidewalks. On some side streets children and adults play on the middle of the street. A basketball court right on the road is a common sight. Horn-blowing is advisable all the time in these cases.

5. Other hazards on the road are bicycle riders, bread vendors on bicycles early before sunrise whose bikes have no lights or reflectors, stray animals, bull carts or calesas (horse-drawn rigs) driven at night without lights or reflectors on highways in the provinces, and pedestrians jaywalking. Drivers are wary about these everytime they take to the road.

6. Rural folk spread their palay to dry right on the middle of roads in the provinces. Drivers slow down when driving over them to avoid accidents.

7. Once in a while, along highways in the provinces at night, drivers come across a "walking house." This is a whole house being transferred to another place on the shoulders of several men in *bayanihan* style, a Filipino custom of community cooperation. Years ago, a Western navy driver killed 3 men and injured 28 others when he ran into a "bayanihan" one night. When driving at night drivers are on the lookout for such activities.

8. In the summer months from March to May, drivers also are forced to exercise extreme patience when they come across parades and processions that occupy the whole width of the road. They have to follow these processions and overtake them only upon being given the "go" signal. The same is true of funeral processions on the road. Blowing the car-horn at this time is considered irreverent, so drivers just have to wait.

9. Rainy months bring in bumpy roads and flooded areas, too, so driving through the floods can be dangerous. Drivers are cautious about the depth of water on the road when they drive on rainy days.

10. When a car breaks down, Filipino drivers put out their early warning device or lift the car hood to signal that the car is out of order. Whenever possible the car is pushed to the right shoulder of the road to make as little obstruction as possible to the flow of traffic.

11. A driver who gets involved in an accident, readily gives assistance to the injured person or if there is no harm inflicted on anyone, he guards the scene of the accident against further

accidents by warning other motorists. He extends cooperation to investigators who come to the scene by giving all pertinent information needed and leaves the place only upon being released by the authorities concerned. In case he has injured a person and he is afraid of being lynched by relatives of the victim, the driver can leave immediately but he must go directly to the nearest police station to report the accident.

12. Drivers of public buses, jeeps and taxis often assume the right of way during peak hours. Filipino drivers are generally aggressive. Defensive driving is, therefore, highly recommended.

Attending Parties in the Philippines

Filipinos are fond of giving parties. Any event can be an excuse for having a small or big party—the baptism of an infant, a birthday, a daughter's debut, or a wedding. Even a promotion in a job, passing a government exam, getting one's first pay check or recovery from illness is reason enough to give a "blow-out." This blow-out may be buying coke and sandwiches for a group of friends or going to an eatery for merienda after office hours.

Giving parties call for etiquette that combine eastern and western practices. There are, however, some peculiar customs that Filipinos observe during parties and the foreigner should be aware of them. A few are explained below:

1. A Filipina housewife or a couple who give a party are often not very sure of the exact number of guests they'll have for their party. This is not only because those invited do not send replies to invitations but also because those invited are free to take along their family or friends to the party. A Westerner knows definitely that she'll have 20 guests that she invited and no others besides. The Filipino hostess prepares for twice or even thrice the number of people she invited. A party for 20, therefore, can easily be one for 40 guests.

2. Although one may not want to invite everyone to a party, a Filipino feels he has to ask everyone casually; otherwise, he has to invite a few friends on the sly so that the uninvited will not feel left out. The person receiving a casual invitation gets the cue when the person inviting him does not insist on his coming.

3. At parties given in Filipino homes, the host is overly

103

solicituous and gives the impression of being unrelaxed. He keeps apologizing for his small house, the heat, and keeps telling his guests to feel at home.

The host keeps apologizing for his house because one's house is a status symbol. Big houses are usually associated with families of means. Westerners have complained that although they have known their Filipino friends for quite some time and have invited them to their own homes, they haven't been invited in return. This is because Filipinos are self-conscious about their houses. This makes them reluctant to invite people, especially foreigners, to their homes. The house must be at its best, i.e., the floors must be well polished, the walls scrubbed; there must be new curtains, etc., before the house is considered worthy of visitors. The self-consciousness becomes greater when a Western visitor is involved. After seeing pictures of European and American homes in foreign magazines on good house-keeping, which Filipino would dare invite an American or European to his house?

4. The hostess rarely helps entertain the guests because she is usually out in the kitchen supervising the cooking. The children, especially the daughters, are expected to do the entertaining. If the daughter sings or plays the piano, she is expected to oblige with a piano selection or a song after a lot of cajoling from the guests. (Incidentally, the Westerner who expects the guests to pay careful attention to the performance is bound to be disappointed. One cannot expect silence. Conversation and noisy laughter go on while the daughter of the house struggles through a piano selection or a song. Perhaps the persistent claps and requests for an encore are meant to make up for the inattention.)

5. Because it is improper to rush to the dinner table when it is announced that dinner is ready, the host and hostess have to go through the painful process of coaxing everyone to start the meal. Children, especially, have been taught by their parents to wait until the announcement has been done several times before they start eating.

6. The host and the hostess usually don't sit with the guests at the dinner table. The guest of honor sits at the head of the table—after much coaxing. He usually insists that a "more important" person be asked to occupy the seat of honor. This might appear strange to the Westerner who expects the hostess to be at the head of the table and seat the guest of honor to her right. The Westerner may also feel uncomfortable in having the Filipino

hostess hovering over him and insisting that he get more of a certain native dish.

7. When the meal is served buffet style, the hostess goes around telling her visitors to go back to the food table and take some more food of their choice. The guest is expected to eat a lot. If he doesn't, the host will feel that his preparations were not good enough. The guest is not supposed to clean up his plate, though, unless he wants to give the impression that he is so hungry he has to eat up everything.

8. It is improper to leave immediately after eating. The guests must stay for a while and mingle with the other guests. Leaving the party immediately after eating may mean that the guest's sole intention in coming was to eat.

Not all parties are held at home. Today, especially in cities and big towns, the more affluent families hold celebrations in plush restaurants and eateries. There the hosts spend more for food and services but are spared the dfficulties of home entertainment and preparation.

In Restaurants

When parties are held in restaurants, the hosts pre-arrange with the management particulars like the food to serve, number of guests, services to be rendered, etc. Guests come in casual attire if it's an informal party or in formal dresses and barong tagalog if its a formal one like a wedding party.

Guests are seated by tables usually ten to a table and courses are served by waiters. When everyone has finished eating, a brief program may follow after which the host pays the bills and the party breaks up.

The host may ask the waiter to gather the clean left-over food from the tables and have them wrapped to be brought home. This is the Filipino custom called *balot* or wrapped.

Some first class Filipino restaurants now encourage people to eat in the native Filipino style—*Kamayan*, meaning eating with bare hands.

Giving Gifts

Almost all occasions that call for parties necessitate the giving of gifts, hence the invited guests usually bring gifts when they attend birthday parties, baptismal parties, wedding anniversary celebrations or wedding parties.

When a gift is thrust into the hostess hands, it is customarily accompanied by a murmured apology, "Sorry, this is all I can afford," or "This is just a little gift. I hope you will like it."

The hostess gently chides the guest for "having taken the trouble," ("*Nag-abala ka pa!*") or "You shouldn't have bothered," or "There's no need for that," and she receives the gift and puts it aside. The Filipino accepts gifts with seeming disclaimers because this is the polite way of doing it. The giver of the gift should not be taken aback by this and think that his gift is not appreciated. The hostess or celebrator does not open the gift immediately and gush over it for fear of embarrassing the giver. The best time to open all gifts is after the party when all guests have gone.

Although the giver has bought his gift at no little cost he makes it appear that it is not good enough. This, for the Filipino, is a way of making the receiver feel that she doesn't owe him a debt of gratitude.

Filipinos are not accustomed to sending "thank you" notes for gifts received as Westerners do. After receiving the gift the receiver waits for an eventful chance to reciprocate in some way.

Tipping

Although the Philippines is not a "tipping" country there are a few Filipinos who practice it. Tipping depends upon where one goes, what he orders, and the service that is given him or what he exacts. If he patronizes luxurious restaurants and wears expensive clothes or if he is critical and difficult to please, greater "compensation" is expected by those who serve him.

One does not tip when there is a sign that says, "No Tipping."

Tipping is an accepted practice with 10 percent being standard. However, many establishments have adopted a 10 percent service charge, so, whatever is left behind on the plate is extra. Additional tipping is optional. Tipping taxi drivers is also optional. Porters are usually tipped a modest amount per baggage.

Smoking and Littering

1. Smoking is not allowed in cinemas, theaters, and public transportation in the Philippines. It is also not allowed in air-conditioned libraries, conference rooms and classrooms.

2. One does not throw cigarette butts, candy wrappers, bus tickets, etc. on the streets or sidewalks. There are receptacles for refuse near bus-stops and along the streets. This is not just a matter of good etiquette—there is a fine for littering.

Going Shopping

Shopping in Manila or in any other part of the Philippines can be an enjoyable experience for a foreigner not only because of the friendly nature of the Filipino but also because the Philippines represents the last bargain center of the Orient. While imported goods are quite expensive, local products make good buys. Among them are textiles like the delicate "piña" and "jusi" material for dresses and barong tagalogs, wood carvings, shell carvings, rattan art, "buntal" hats, abaca placemats, rugs and bags, Philippine cigars, antique *santos*, black coral, inlaid brass and bronzeware, gold and silver filigree work and other costume jewelry.

Principal shopping centers in Manila and other big cities are open the whole week from 9:00 a.m. to 7:00 p.m. Goods are sold at fixed prices so no bargaining takes place in these big stores.

In smaller shops and stores, however, bargaining or *tawad* system is practiced. This is a form of buying in which the buyer asks verbally for a discount in price of the goods he likes to buy. Haggling starts from around 30 to 40 percent of the usual price and goes on until finally the seller gives the goods at a much lower price than the previous one given.

The expatriate must learn words and expressions like tawad, *"Mahal ito* (It's expensive)," *"Magkano ito?* (How much does this cost)?" so that he can get a good buy. Establishing a personalized relationship with the seller, showing a warm feeling towards him, always works toward getting a good discount.

Marketing and Sales Practices

Marketing and sales practices of Filipinos are strange and interesting. Among the more common ones are the following:

1. The *suki* habit—This is a traditional buying practice of Filipinos which must have been introduced by the Chinese because suki is a Chinese word. Here the buyer patronizes one store instead of buying from different stores at different times. The store owner in return obliges by giving discounts or extra little things as *dagdag* or addition. These may be extra spices, two extra pieces of candies, etc. all to entice the buyer to continue buying from his store. It is worth noting, though, that Chinese cornerstore owners practice this more than any other seller, Filipino or other nationalities.

2. Sellers always take note of the very first person to buy their goods in the morning. This buyer gets a discount on whatever she buys because she is *buena mano* or the good hand, being the first for the day. She is supposed to bring about a good sale for the whole day. Some sellers believe that some persons are good buena manos while others are not depending on how brisk their sale goes after that first purchase.

3. The *lako* or peddling system is practiced everywhere in the Philippines. Peddlers carry their wares which may be fish, meat, vegetables, fruits and other food, jewelry, even furniture and bring them right at the doorstep of buyers. They make their presence known by shouting aloud announcing what they have for sale. While prices here may be a bit higher than those in the market, many housewives buy from them because it saves them the trouble of going on trips outside their homes.

4. In the public markets, some sellers use the *tumpok-tumpok* system of selling. Fruits, vegetables, small fishes in small piles or *tumpok* are lined up and sold at lower prices. The average market-going housewife usually buys from these vendors because it is easier for them to estimate the amount needed for the size of their families.

5. A unique buying habit among the fishermen and buyers in Parañaque and Malabon (fishing towns within Metro Manila) is the *bulungan* (literally translated "whispering"). Early in the morning before sunrise, buyers who are mostly fishmongers from different markets meet the fishermen on the shore while they are still unloading their bountiful catch. Prospective buyers approach the fisherman one at a time and will break the ice by speaking in the language of the fisherman. A fisherman is approached by the buyer by buzzing or whispering into his ears the amount he wants to pay for the fish. The fisherman already knows what price he wants for his commodity. If the amount offered does not meet his expectations, the buyer may whisper another price quotation and if still unacceptable the "bulungan" continues to other buyers. Another buyer will come to the fisherman and will follow the same method of procuring fish. This bulungan is continued until the seller hears the best price. If, for instance, all the buyers have approached the fisherman and still no agreement is made about the selling price of the fish, then the latter will sell his fish to the buyer who offered him the highest price for his catch.

6. Buying and selling using *kantahan* or singing as medium of communication is heard among fish vendors in markets. Each seller tries to attract the attention of buyers with her singing, trying to outsing and outsell her neighbor vendor.

7. In market eateries or food sections it is not uncommon to see lady waitresses holding customers by their hands pulling them into their eatery to eat their food for sale.

8. "Hi! Joe. Wanna buy watch?" This is a gimmick sometimes used in cities. A mestizo dressed in a U.S. Navy uniform offers to sell a watch or two at a low price because he's "about to leave for the U.S." Buyers of these watches are sometimes cheated because they are actually of the poorest quality. Ignorant provincianos and gullible city-dwellers fall easy prey to this gimmick.

9. When a foreign-looking buyer comes around, sellers usually jack-up their prices believing that Westerners have much money and can afford to pay goods at higher prices.

10. Many Filipinos love to buy by installment or *hulugan* and *paiyakan*. This is common in offices, schools or even in neighborhoods where periodic payments for goods bought are collected by the sellers. Although goods get higher in price because of the installment plan, it is resorted to by many who cannot afford to

pay big amounts in cash for furniture, appliances and jewelry. It enables them to "keep up with the Perezes."

Business Hours

Ordinary office hours in the country are from 8:00 a.m. to 5:00 p.m. Banking hours are from 9:00 a.m. to 4:00 p.m.

Office hours for business and commercial centers start at 9:00 a.m. and end at 6:00 p.m.

These office hours differ due to the fact that business or commercial centers cater to the general public while ordinary offices cater to clients and in-company personnel. Banks close early at 4:00 p.m. because employees have clearing processes to do.

Philippine Currency

The Philippine official monetary unit is the peso which is equivalent to 100 centavos.

Coins of one, two and five peso denominations, and one, five, ten, twenty-five and fifty centavo denominations are used all over the country.

Paper bills are in two, five, ten, twenty, fifty and one hundred peso denominations.

The exchange rate for foreign currency tends to fluctuate but as a guide, the U.S. dollar rate of exchange is the basis of reference. Foreign currency may be changed to pesos in commercial banks and foreign exchange dealers authorized by the Central Bank of the Philippines.

Traveller's cheques may be cashed in all commercial banks in the Philippines and are accepted in most hotels, restaurants and shops.

There is no limit to foreign currency being brought into the country. However, foreign currency to be taken out of the country must not exceed an amount determined also by the Central Bank of the Philippines.

PART THREE

LIVING IN THE PHILIPPINES

9 OVERCOMING STRESS FACTORS

Every culture is unique and each has its own set of value systems. Even very closely related cultures still have some very unique features which differentiate one from the others. Sometimes, one finds out these differences only when already in a new culture setting. This is culture shock!

The Nature of Culture Shock

Culture shock is the state of difficulty of coping with the new or different culture. It is a sort of an occupational sickness of someone who has been suddenly transferred abroad. JoAnn Craig describes it as the feeling of being a fish out of water.[24] It is the feeling of distress and uneasiness in the new environment caused primarily by a loss of cues. Cues are familiar signs and symbols which help one cope with the formal circumstances of life such as how to eat, how to address and greet a person, when to accept and when to refuse offered food, when to offer one's seat to a lady and when not to offer. For example, in Indonesia pointing with your index finger is considered an insult. In the Arab states, one should never shake hands using the left hand. They consider the left hand to be unclean. The list could go on and on. Thus, an individual who finds himself in a totally different culture without adequate preparation and training, will very likely be a victim of culture shock. The great French philosopher-mathematician Pascal once said: "There are truths on this side of the Pyrenees that are falsehoods on the other."

Culture shock is the more pronounced reaction to the psychological disorientation most people experience when they move for an extended period of time into a culture markedly different from their own. It is different from frustration which is traceable to a specific action or cause and goes away when the situation is remedied or the cause is removed. Some common causes of frustration are the ambiguity of a particular situation, the actual situation not matching preconceived ideas of what it would be like, unrealistic goals, not being able to see results or using the wrong methods to achieve objectives. Frustration is related to culture shock and similar in emotional content. However, it is generally short-lived as compared to culture shock.

Culture shock is caused by being cut off from the cultural cues and known patterns with which one is familiar. It comes from the experience of encountering ways of doing, organizing, perceiving or valuing things which are different from ours and which threaten our basic, unconscious belief that our acculturated customs, assumptions, values and behaviors are "right."

Culture shock builds up slowly from a series of small events which are difficult to identify. It comes from living and/or working over an extended period of time in a situation that is ambiguous. It comes from having one's own values which he has considered as absolutes brought into question.

Culture shock comes in progressive stages:

First stage: Initial Euphoria. One who goes to work in another culture begins with great expectations and a positive mind-set. At this point, anything new is exciting. However, for the most part, the similarities stand out. This stage may last from a week or two to a month.

Second stage: Irritation and Hostility. In this stage the focus of attention is on the differences. Insignificant difficulties become major catastrophies. This is the stage identified as "culture shock." Symptoms of this state are homesickness, boredom, withdrawal, need for excessive amounts of sleep, compulsive eating, compulsive drinking, irritability, exaggerated cleanliness, marital stress, family tension and conflict, chauvinistic excesses, stereotyping of host nationals, hostility toward host nationals, loss of ability to work effectively, unexplainable fits of weeping and psychosomatic illnesses.

Third stage: Gradual Adjustment. Once one begins to orient himself and is able to interpret some of the subtle cultural clues and cues which passed by unnoticed earlier, the culture seems more familiar. In this stage the crisis is over and one is recovering from the shock. One becomes more comfortable in the culture and feels less isolated from it. One starts to realize that the situation is not so bad after all and starts to have a sense of humor.

Fourth stage: Adaptation or Biculturalism. This is the stage of full recovery, resulting in an ability to function in two cultures with confidence. One becomes acculturated and finds the host country's culture, customs, values and traditions great.

Guidelines for Cross-Cultural Orientation and Adjustment

One of the best actions to overcome culture shock is to know as much as possible about the culture of the country where one is. One should search assiduously and consciously for logical reasons behind everything in the host culture which seems strange, difficult, confusing, or threatening. He should find patterns and interrelationships. Finding the logical explanation behind the things one observes in the host culture will facilitate positive attitude and empathy with the host culture.

One should never disparage the host culture. Commenting negatively on the host culture will just add to his unhappiness. He should talk and deal closely with the host nationals whom he has identified as sympathetic and understanding to him. He should have faith in the inherent and essential goodwill of his country and the positive outcome of his experience.

It is advisable to study the following aspects of the host culture:

A. *Social customs:*

1. The character of the people
2. Formal and informal greeting forms
3. Appropriate manners in entering a house
4. Appropriate manners when shopping
5. Appropriate manners at the theater
6. Appropriate manners in a beauty shop
7. Appropriate manners in entering a room

115

8. Appropriate moment in a new relationship to give one's name, ask the other's name, inquire about occupation or family.
9. Appropriate manners for husband and wife
10. Expected gesture of appreciation for an invitation to a home
11. Appropriate manners in giving and receiving gifts
12. Appropriate way and place of sitting
13. Appropriate ways of showing respect
14. Appropriate ways in attending weddings, funerals, baptisms, birthdays, or other official ceremonies
15. Appropriate manners when talking with someone
16. Appropriate way of escorting someone across the street
17. Appropriate reactions to laughing, crying, fainting or blushing in a group situation
18. Particular facial expressions or gestures considered rude
19. Concept of proper personal grace.
20. Concept of "personal" questions
21. Punctuality required for social and business appointments
22. Appropriate way of calling the attention of a waiter in a restaurant
23. Appropriate way of refusing an invitation without offending
24. Appropriate manner of expressing condolence when death occurs
25. Appropriate response when an unknown person in apparent need comes to ask for help

B. *Family Life:*

1. Basic unit of social organization
2. Members of the family whom you expect to meet when invited to a home
3. Proper greetings for the adults and elderly
4. Role of women
5. Duties of men and women in the family
6. Arrangements for offspring's and widow's inheritance
7. Toys and games ascribed to boys and girls
8. Teaching techniques used at home and in school to correct disapproved behavior

9. Important events in family life and ways of celebrating them
10. Ceremony to mark passage from childhood to adulthood
11. Responsibilities in wedding ceremonies
12. Approved encounters between sexes prior to marriage
13. Forms of marriages (polygamy, monogamy, divorce)
14. Symbols used in marriage

C. *Housing, Clothing and Food:*

1. Functions served by the average dwelling (toileting, cooking, etc.)
2. Differences in the kinds of housing used by different social groups
3. Textiles, colors or decorations identified with specific social or occupation groups
4. Special dresses required for different occasions
5. Types of clothing considered taboo for one or the other sex
6. Parts of the body that must always be covered by clothing
7. Customary number of meals a day
8. Proper habits in eating
9. Unique food eaten only in that country
10. Food for ceremonies and festivals
11. Prestige food
12. Food and drinks indicative of appropriate hospitality for relatives, close friends, official acquaintances and strangers
13. Setting a good table for social recognition
14. The seat of honor when dining

D. *Class Structure:*

1. Classes in society
2. Racial, religious or economic factors which determine social status
3. Birth as predeterminant factor of status
4. Different class structures in rural and urban areas
5. Individuals and families of predominant social position
6. Particular roles or activities appropriate or inappropriate to the status in which one's nationality is classified

E. *Political Patterns:*

1. Immediate outside threats to the political survival of the country
2. Manifestations of political power
3. Channels opened for the expression of popular opinion
4. Sources of media information
5. Political structures for the cities
6. Ways of handling international representation and foreign policies
7. Profile of and center of power structure
8. Politics in social situation and appropriate behavior on the part of a foreigner
9. Channels available to opposition groups

F. *Religion and Folk Beliefs:*

1. Predominant religious group
2. Fundamental religious beliefs on man, life after death, source of evil, nature of the Deity
3. Religious beliefs influencing daily activities
4. Hierarchy of religious functionaries of institutionalized religion
5. Places, objects, events, festivals and writings possessing sacred values
6. Tolerance for minority religions
7. Exorcism of evil spirits
8. Ceremonies done to insure good fortune to a new child or enterprise or building
9. Objects and actions that portend good luck or bad luck
10. Myths taught to children as part of their cultural heritage

G. *Economic Institutions:*

1. Geographic location and climate affecting the ways food, clothing and shelter are provided
2. Available natural resources and things imported
3. Foodstuffs imported
4. GNP, principal products, major exports and imports
5. Basic items not available in the market; luxury items available
6. Available technological training

7. Organizations of industrial and rural workers
8. Cooperatives' importance to the economy
9. Significance of multinational corporations; types of businesses
10. Percentage of population engaged in agriculture, in industry, in service trades
11. Protections developed against natural disasters
12. Definitions of virtues and vices
13. Definitions of work and play

H. *Arts:*

1. Media for artistic expression
2. Professional artists and art schools
3. Most used materials
4. Art objects typically found in homes, in museums
5. Kind of music and musical instruments unique to the country
6. Popular forms of drama and dance
7. Specific songs for special occasions

I.. *Value System:*

1. View of life
2. View on competition and cooperation
3. View on thriftiness and life enjoyment
4. View on work
5. View on self-esteem (face or fact?)
6. View on truth (politeness or factual honesty?)
7. View on the destiny of man
8. View on capital punishment, war, killing of adulterers, infanticide during famine, euthanasia or mercy-killing
9. Definition of a "friend" and responsibilities of friendship
10. Injunctions taught to children
11. Traditional heroes and heroines, popular idols of the day and values symbolized by them

J. *Others:*

1. Common form of marriage: civil, church, common-law
2. Ways of spending leisure time
3. Favorite recreational activities of the people

4. Attitude toward gambling
5. Types of films shown at local movie theaters
6. Money used. Common denominations of bills and coins. Exchange rate for U.S. dollar
7. Normal mealtime schedules
8. Foods that are taboo
9. Circumstances where smoking is permitted
10. Availability of physicians' services
11. Normal dress of men and women
12. Standards of public hygiene and sanitation
13. Literary rate of the population
14. Presence of children at social concerns
15. History of relationships between the host country and the expatriate country

Comparing and Contrasting Cultures

There are five basic questions that get at the root of any culture's value system, no matter how different or seemingly exotic. They are the following:[26]

1. The Human Nature Orientation: What is the character of innate human nature?
2. The Man-Nature Question: What is the relation of Man to Nature?
3. The Time Orientation Question: What is the temporal focus (time sense) of human life?
4. The Activity Orientation Question: What is the mode of human activity?
5. The Social Orientation Question: What is the mode of human relationships?

In terms of the *values* found in answering these questions, let us analyze the Kluckholm Model:

Comparative Values and Beliefs

Orientation	Range		
Human Nature	Most people can't be trusted.	There are both evil people and good people in the world. And you have to check people out to find out which they are.	Most people are basically pretty good at heart.
Man-Nature Relationship	Life is largely determined by external forces such as God, Fate or Genetics. A person can't surpass the conditions life has set.	Man should in every way live in complete harmony with nature.	Man's challenge is to conquer and control nature. Everything from air conditioning to the Green Revolution has resulted from having met this challenge.
Time Sense	Man should learn from history and attempt to emulate the glorious ages of the past.	The present moment is everything. Let's make the most of it. Don't worry about tomorrow. Enjoy today.	Planning and goal setting make it possible for man to accomplish miracles. A little sacrifice today will bring a better tomorrow.
Activity	It's enough to just "be." It's not necessary to accomplish great things in life to feel your life has been worthwhile.	Man's main purpose for being placed on this earth is for one's own inner development.	If people work hard and apply themselves fully, their efforts will be rewarded.
Social Relations	Some people are born to lead others. There are "leaders" and there are "followers" in this world.	Whenever I have a serious problem, I like to get the advice of my family or close friends on how best to solve it.	All people should have equal rights and each should have complete control over one's own destiny.

An Exercise for the Expatriate

Using this comparison model, analyze your culture and that of your host culture. Where did you find your own culture? To the left, center or right or the continuum? Where did you find your host culture? To the left, center or right or the continuum? Most Westerners find their values to the *right* of it while most Orientals find their values to the *left* of it. With good judgment and careful observation, you can identify your own views and values and compare them with those of the host country as relative positions on the dimensions of continuous variability between opposite extreme poles, shown below:[27]

A. *Defining Activity*

1. Who should make decisions?
    senior authorities . . . . majority of the people
                                                          affected
2. How do people regard and handle work?
    a means to other ends . . . . an end in itself
    a burden . . . . a challenge
    coping with situations . . . . solving problems
                                                          planning
3. How do people evaluate activity?
    goals, ideals . . . . techniques, projects
                                                          procedures
4. How do people evaluate activity?
    being . . . . . becoming . . . . . . doing
    fatalistic . . . . striving
    slow pace, easy going . . . . fast pace, compulsive

B. *Defining Social Relations*

1. How do people relate to others with different statuses?
    stress differences . . . . stress equality
    stress formality . . . . stress informality
2. How are roles defined and allocated?
    ascribed . . . . . attained . . . . . achieved
    explicit . . . . implicit
    sex roles distinct . . . . sex roles similar
3. How do people communicate with others?
    indirectly, through

        intermediaries . . . . directly
        communion . . . . communication
    4. What is the basis for social control and conformity?
        shame . . . . guilt
        authority, status . . . . impersonal rules, laws
    5. How do people handle their emotions?
        restrain, suppress . . . . express openly
    6. How is social reciprocity defined?
        ideal and real . . . . real only

C. *Defining the Self*

    1. How should a person form his identity?
        with others . . . . by oneself
        spiritual . social . achievements . possessions
        life . . . . . . positions . . . . . .
    2. What is the nature of individualism?
        duties . . . . rights
        personal commitment . . . . personal commitment
            not stressed   stressed
        self-interests . . . . self-interests
        overtly stated   covertly stated
        companionship . . . . privacy

One way of getting the basic cultural values of a host country is to gather their proverbs and translate them into their value content. Take the proverb "Early to bed, early to rise, makes a man healthy, wealthy, and wise" which means the value of diligence or work ethic. Study also the concepts that shape the "way of life" of your host culture. Take the concept "Time is Money." This teaches that time is a material thing and that it should be actively mastered or manipulated to one's advantage. The characteristics of the host country's way of life is a set of values that differentiates them from other peoples of the world. These values are largely a product of the host country's culture. Since one's cultural values influence his behavior in no small measure, anyone who would attempt to understand the Filipinos' behavior will have to familiarize himself with Philippine cultural values.

An important part of human behavior is reaction to the pictures in their heads. Human behavior takes place in relation to a pseudo-environment—a representation which is not quite the same for any two individuals. This man-made cultural environment, which has its being in the minds of men is interposed between man as a biological organism and the external reality. We must bring the "pictures in the mind" and "external reality" into truer alignment, through first-hand experiences, audio-visual representations, and words. It is through words, however, that most of our cultural orientation and adjustment take place and much is inevitably lost in the telling as word descriptions are substituted for their real-life counterparts. Consider words such as good, bad, ugly, beautiful, moral, immoral. Dictionaries carry definitions but people carry connotations—and it is connotations which rule thinking and influence behavior. To facilitate cultural orientation, the following are some guidelines:[28]

1. No two things are identical, and no one thing remains the same. For example: Filipino, is not Filipino, is not Filipino, is not Filipino . . . In other words Filipino (Jose Rizal) is not Filipino (Andres Bonifacio) is not Filipino (Farmer in a rural barrio) . . . Although by convention we refer to the fifty million people who live in an area called Philippines as "Filipinos," the truth is that no two Filipinos are identical. Statements which purport to talk about "the Filipinos" as if they were one entity; must be carefully qualified. Questions like "What do Filipinos think about Americans?" become clearly unanswerable.

2. The same word may be used to connote different "realities," while similar events or experiences are sometimes called by different names. For example, a term like "parliamentary" is used by many to describe political systems like those of the United Kingdom, Philippines, etc. which first-hand examination reveals as quite dissimilar.

3. Statements of opinion are often confused with statements of facts. For example "cold wave" could mean anything from 20 or 30 degree below zero (F) in the Himalayas to 40 degrees above in New Delhi. We can differentiate opinions from facts by adding the words "to me" or "to you."

4. It is not possible to tell about anything. All descriptions are "open-ended" with the last word unsaid. Thus, for example, an examination of Filipinism might include reference to Filipino values, ideals, and so on, but no matter how extensive the treatise is, a mental "etc." should be added to the last punctuation point.

5. Try to use descriptive terms rather than those expressing

approval or disapproval. For example, the words "clean" and "unclean" are relative. Vermiculture or raising worms for some women may be "unclean."

6. Try to use phrases which indicate certain conditions which should be considered with a statement. For example, awareness may be increased by using such phrases as "in our culture," "from my point of view," or "at that time."

7. Try to move in the direction of substituting more precise words for vague ones.

8. Become more alert to the ways in which cultural conditioning shapes one's value judgments.

9. Become more suspicious of one's own "wisdom."

Community Study

To understand fully the host culture and its people, one of the best things to do is to make a community study. Below is an outline in making a community study.

OUTLINE OF A COMMUNITY STUDY

I. INTRODUCTION
II. COMMUNITY IDENTIFICATION
  1. The first impressions of the place, the first "look-see" appearance as one approaches it and its general location relative to other places
  2. Landmarks
III. THE ECOLOGICAL FRAME
  1. Geographical factors
  2. Population make-up
  3. Climate and soil
  4. Service institutions
  5. Town plan
  6. Government
IV. HISTORICAL DEVELOPMENT
  1. Origin
  2. First inhabitants
  3. Development
  4. Conversion into a barrio, or town, or subdivision, etc.
  5. Progress at present
V. LIFE ACTIVITIES
  1. Social structure: social status of the residents
  2. Daytime activities
  3. Social relationships

125

    4. Favorite pastime and recreation

    5. Saturday and Sunday nights activities

    6. Groups and organizations: date and founder, members, aims, nature, activities

VI. COMPLEX OF VALUES

    1. Core values of the community, that is, those that are generally accepted in society

    2. Aim values of the community, that is, those options that society allows its members

    3. Attitudes and sense of values

VII. GROUP CONFLICTS AND PROBLEMS

    1. Controversies: nature, reasons and causes, etc.

    2. Factions: political, religious, etc.

    3. Problems: moral, spiritual, religious, water problem, garbage, sanitation, security, toilet, etc.

VIII. IMPACT OF THE WORLD OUTSIDE

    1. The inflow of ideas, goods, special forms, moral codes, new *modus vivendi et operandi* from the outside world to the community

    2. Physical changes caused by this impact (world to the community)

    3. Spiritual and moral changes in the way of life conduct and activities of the members of the community

    4. Change in attitudes and values

    5. Other changes caused by the impact

IX. GOODNESS OF LOCAL LIFE

    1. The goodness or badness of the community from the liability point of view: "Is it a good place to stay in?"

    2. Good aspects of the community

    3. Bad aspects of the community

X. CONCLUSION

    1. Observations

    2. Recommendations and suggestions

    3. Community project for this coming summer

XI. BIBLIOGRAPHY

    1. Books and journals, newsletter, etc.

    2. Miscellaneous entries: Survey Forms, Barrio Charter resolutions, etc.

    3. Persons interviewed and co-researchers

XII. APPENDIX

    1. Pictures, etc.

    2. Maps

    3. Xerox copy of the important documents such as the barrio resolutions

Cross-Cultural Orientation and Adjustment

Training in the management of different cultures is important because culture shock has suddenly become an urgent issue with many expatriates in another culture. Alcoholism, drug abuse, falling off of work performance, steady build-up of complaints and sickness absences are indicators that one is not oriented and adjusted in the culture where he is.

Philip Harris suggests four components in an effective policy for expatriates:[29] (a) selection of people for overseas postings since not all are suitable, (b) orientation before they go, (c) monitoring them while they are abroad and the provision of support services to them and their families, (d) the re-entry process, which includes assisting them before they leave their overseas posts and on their return.

There are certain qualities necessary for getting along in other cultures such as the capacity to communicate, respect, positive regard, encouragement and sincere interest. An expatriate should recognize that everyone's point of view is relative rather than absolute. These points should be emphasized in cross-cultural orientation preparing people for overseas assignments. Good cross-cultural orientation and preparation can cut the costs of culture-shocked staff. A systematic training in cultural differences is necessary before personnel are posted in a job of another culture to enable them to cope effectively with that foreign culture.

It is necessary for Westerners to adapt to the Filipino sense of time, place and face. The Philippines is populated by multi-cultured and multi-lingual people speaking different languages and over a dozen dialects. A Westerner who is jet-propelled from a so-called advanced technological society into a developing agricultural society should be aware that all the things he has *taken* for granted are not available in the society where he is going: instant and good communication facilities, good transportation facilities, good traffic management, etc. All his reference points are off.

Before any employee is sent overseas a three-day cultural awareness workshop should be conducted focusing on the concept and characteristics of culture and how to analyze a culture. The skills needed for succeeding in overcoming culture shock and for good cross-cultural adjustment are openmindedness, nonjudgmentalness, empathy, tolerance for ambiguity, communicativeness, flexibility, curiosity, sense of humor, warmth in human relationships, self-motivation, strong sense of self and perceptiveness. One should have a relaxed attitude toward personal status, time pressures, minor hardships and inconveniences. To be adjusted in another culture one should have a sense of self comfortable enough that he can stick to his own judgments under stress but can also yield and compromise when flexibility is needed. He should have a strong family relationship, genuine friendliness, ingenuity or ability to go around roadblocks, a desire to understand people, inner resourcefulness and zest for the unknown.

Dealing with Stress

To be well adjusted and happy in another culture, one must develop the following transcultural skills:[30]

1. *Respect.* One who lives in another culture should acquire the skill of communicating respect; that is to say, of transmitting both verbally and non-verbally positive regard, encouragement, and sincere interest in the other's culture.

2. *Impartiality.* One who lives in another culture should be non-judgmental in one's behavior and responses. It means avoiding moralistic, value-laden statements. Impartiality is the optimal energizer of openness.

3. *Interiorization.* One who lives in another culture should learn to personalize knowledge and perceptions. He should recognize and be aware of the influence of his own values, perceptions, opinion and knowledge in his interactions with others. The learning in cross-cultural relations has become a part of the self.

4. *Empathy.* One who lives in another culture should display empathy in his behavior and therefore strive to understand others from *their* point of view. Empathy is putting into action the effort to enter into the other's perceptions and world of values and reacting accordingly. This is perhaps one of the most difficult yet highest expression of cross-cultural adaptation for it entails no small measure of forgetfulness of the self and interest in the self of the other.

5. *Flexibility.* This skill is adaptability to the others. Flexibility, in a way, is the offshoot of the other previous four skills made operational.

6. *Mutuality.* One who lives in another culture should demon-

strate reciprocal concern among the parties involved in transcultural communication. They maintain the dialogue by taking turns talking, sharing, and interacting responsibly. If they are part of a group, they promote circular communication. This type of communication by its very nature forgets bonds of new communities through new relationships discovered.

7. *Suspense.* One who lives in another culture should tolerate ambiguity. Respect, impartiality, empathy, and flexibility coming and acting together produce that open attitude that suspends judgments, opens up options and allows for deeper inter-communication between individuals or groups of differing cultures. Suspense therefore, enables the parties involved to cope with cultural differences, and to accept a certain degree of frustration.

Adjusting to new surroundings, a new job, and a new culture, and acquiring a supportive network of friends cause stress and mental anxiety. Not knowing how to handle and manage stress, may lead one to alcoholism, drug abuse or even overeating. Common problems which expatriates experience in their home countries such as marital stress and problems with their children are sometimes accentuated due to new setting. Idle wives of expatriates who have nothing to do due to abundance of household help or who do not have a working visa or permit suffer some self-esteem crises.

Symptoms of stress are: severe physiological or psychological fatigue, prolonged periods of general anxiety, worry or brooding, unrelieved distress or brooding over a specific problem or defeat in business or personal life, general feeling that one is not performing as well as he could, feeling that problems in one's life are getting beyond one's control, general difficulties in getting along with other people, serious difficulty in getting along with a certain person one can't avoid, worrying that other people or a certain person doesn't like him or are "out to get" him, an unexplained increase in family problems, general feelings of unhappiness or dissatisfaction with life, a feeling of failure, or brooding over goals that he has not achieved and probably will never achieve, brooding over death and recurring thoughts of suicide.

A family physician who has some knowledge of psychiatry, may be able to help or he can probably refer him to a qualified expert for advice. Other sources of help in cases of stress are the following: local medical societies, professional associations of psychiatrists or psychologists, psychiatric hospitals or clinics, general hospitals with a psychiatric department, mental health associations, community mental health centers, medical schools, psychology departments of colleges and universities, psychological consulting organizations.

Overcoming Effects of Culture Shock

Since a meeting of a new culture will almost always result in a culture shock, what can be done to smooth the transition? First and foremost, one must learn to take into his consideration the values, idiosyncracies and "quirks" that the new culture exhibit. The newly arrived Westerner must learn to be less ethnocentric. He should spend more time with the people of the new culture to have understanding, awareness and appreciation that will pave the way to acceptance and adaptation. He should be adequately prepared through some form of cultural awareness intervention.

This cultural awareness intervention can be done in an in-country training. In this way pitfalls in observing local customs can be avoided.

10 THE EXPATRIATE IN THE PHILIPPINES

Expatriates are foreign nationals who have lived and worked in a third-world foreign country for more than six months, who consider their country of residence as alien, and their country of origin as home.[31] They move from one place to another and have no real place to call home. Their style of life is exposed to the "shock" of the foreign culture they live in and to the "shock" of living the "Expatriate Lifestyle." What are some of the problems that they encounter in living overseas? What can they do to get over culture shock as quickly as possible? What are some of the pleasures and benefits of the expatriate life?

Problems of Expatriates

The problems encountered by expatriates in living overseas are of several categories. The first category is the problem of *emotional nature*. Feelings such as depression, anxiety, disorientation, distraction, irritability, homesickness and loneliness are some of the emotional problems encountered by expatriates once they are uprooted and transplanted into an alien culture. A natural outcome of such emotional problem is excessive drinking.

Another category of expatriates' problem is that pertaining to *life-style*. Things such as cultural differences, stranger anxiety, competition with foreign enterprise, problems with wives and separation from one's family are some of these problems. They encounter problems in understanding the local culture, its value system, its work attitudes, and its business structures. They often

131

experience distress in their own inability to cross the cultural curtain. They are handicapped by the very nature of their operation as "foreign" enterprises. They lack the behavioral know-how in treating local employees to make their foreign operation successful. Marital problems also have a tendency to multiply because of the stress of an unfamiliar and non-supportive culture. Some expatriates' wives and children are unable to "settle in." When the wife cannot adjust, family problems spill over into the business life of the expatriate husband.

Separation from the family causes extreme loneliness to some expatriates. Losing touch with their own family and culture causes them great pain.

An expatriate woman's life-style changes dramatically when she moves into a foreign country. While in her country of origin, she was living the comfortable middle class level, she finds herself now living in the upper or middle-upper classes of the new environment. While way back home there was a big separation of home life and work life, now she finds herself involved in a whirl of entertaining and socializing as part of her functions as an executive's wife. Furthermore, her personal behavior is no longer a matter of private concern but a reflection on her husband and his company. If the husband has to travel much, the wife often has to face long periods of loneliness and perhaps insecurity depending on the geographical location of their residence.

Some expatriate wives may miss their financial independence since they can't work nor be gainfully employed in the host country. This is further aggravated by the fact that boredom may attack them since in the Philippines they have all the help needed at home such as servants, cooks, drivers and gardeners. Used to working hard and using their minds in their country of origin, they are now confronted with the problem of how to make use of too much time in their hands.

Some women encounter problems on how to handle their servants. They also need to learn the cultural values of these servants in order to get along well with them.

The children of expatriates do encounter some problems, too. They have new habits to learn, new behavioral expectations, new customs, new people and new ways of "modus operandi" and "modus vivendi." They have to cope with a new school system and a new social life.

132

The Coping Process

To get over culture impact as quickly as possible an expatriate must understand the *accommodation process*, that is, the skill or procedure that an individual calls upon in getting along with other people, with institutions and with the society where he lives. Synonymous to the accommodation process are the coping process or the adapting process. The expatriate should understand that throughout life there are circumstances in which one cannot have his own way. The purposes and desires of another person or a group of people or an institution are in the forefront. He must weigh his own needs, consider the other demands and then implement behavior that maintains harmony.

Basic to skill in accommodation is the capability of the individual to know himself, to have integrated his experiences and be able to say this is me, my competencies and liabilities, my desires and wants, my needs, my idiosyncracies. In this perspective, the expatriate sizes up the dimensions of the "other" system whether it be a person, a society, or an institution. He does not have control over the other situation, but potentially has control over his own person. He must decide what behavior to employ to bring about the desired outcomes. To do this, he must learn as much as he can about the customs, the habits, the culture, the patterns of everyday behavior, the manners, the attitudes and the idiosyncracies of the people of the Philippines. Once he realizes that the trouble of culture shock is due to his *own* lack of communicating with the cues, signs and symbols of his own culture, rather than the hostility of an alien environment, he will realize that he himself can gain this understanding and the means to social intercourse through study and learning.[32]

Unfortunately very few multinational corporations in the Philippines give cultural orientation to their expatriates. Thus, one must have his own initiative in taking classes in the culture and languages of the host country whenever possible. The universities and some training agencies such as the Philippine Institute of Tourism often offer classes to which the public are invited. Values and Technologies Management Center conducts cross-cultural seminars in the Philippines for expatriates of multinational organizations. The expatriate should talk to the locals as much as possible, ask them to teach him the dos and don'ts, the whys and the hows. He should read books to help him understand the Filipino psyche. Some titles are suggested here:

1. *Understanding Values* — Tomas D. Andres
2. *Understanding the Filipino and His Values* — Tomas D. Andres
3. *Philippines* — Sylvia Mayuga, Alfred Yuson et al.
4. *Understanding the Filipino Migrants*
5. *The Filipinos Take a Second Look at Themselves* — Delfin Batacan
6. *Filipino Thought on Man and Society* — Fr. L. Mercado
7. *Church of the Philippines on the Threshold of the 80's* — Jesus Fernandez, S.J. and the editorial staff, Philippine Priests, Inc.
8. *Filipino Women and Other Essays* — Carmen Guerrero Nakpil
9. *Industrial Promotion Policies in the Philippines*
10. *Doing Business in the Philippines* — SGV and Co.
11. *Question of Identity* — Carmen Guerrero Nakpil
12. *Toward the Restructuring of Filipino Values* — O C R, PA.
13. *Split-Level Christianity* — Jaime Bulatao, S.J.
14. *Four Readings on Philippine Values* — Frank Lynch, S.J.
15. *The Filipino in the Seventies: An Ecumenical Perspective* — Vitaliano R. Gorospe and Richard L. Deats
16. *Management by Filipino Values* — Tomas D. Andres

A Westerner who comes to the Philippines for the first time may be pleasantly surprised to find that he is not in a totally strange world. The term "Westerner" refers here to people from European nations and those of the United States of America, Canada, Australia, New Zealand and others. He sees Filipinos as short, brown-skinned people who speak English, wear Western clothes, go to see Hollywood movies, eat Western dishes, listen to Western music and read Western books. In short, they do what the average Westerner does.

The Filipino: A Cultural Hybrid

The Filipino is a cultural hybrid. Very often a Westerner finds difficulty in distinguishing a Filipino from a Thai, a Malay,

134

a Chinese, a Japanese, a Puerto Rican, a Mexican or a South American.

The Filipinos as a people are one of the most heterogenous groups in the world. To begin with, they are scattered all over 7,000 islands that comprise the archipelago. The islands are divided into regions so distinct from each other that the people speak around 70 different dialects. The dialects are also distinct from each other, so distinct that even neighboring provinces have different meanings for similar words in their dialects.

For example, the word *ibon* means "bird" to the Tagalog-speaking Filipinos, but it means "egg" to the Pampango-speaking Filipinos. To the Tagalogs, *wala* means "there is none," but to the people in Pangasinan, a province in the island of Luzon, it means "there is." There are several other examples that make conversation in the Philippine dialects quite interesting and amusing, sometimes even embarrassing.

The Filipino English

In the Philippines almost everyone speaks English. The average Filipino speaks English well, sometimes even sounding like an American. At times, however, Filipinos speak English with distinct regional accents—Tagalog, Ilocano, Pampango, Visayan—depending on what part of the country the speaker comes from. If the Westerner tries hard enough, he eventually gets used to the staccato rhythm, the peculiar intonation and the irregularities in the use of vowels and consonants brought about by the interference of the use of their dialects.

The Westerner also gets used to the grammatical errors committed by the Filipino. He learns not to be shocked when he hears a Filipino refer to Mrs. Jones as *he* or to Mr. Carter as *she*. Even the most careful and most knowledgeable Filipino speaker of English sometimes misuses his *she's* and *he's* because in his native language there is no such distinction in gender.

Many Filipinos commit errors in tenses when they speak in English. It is not uncommon to hear, for example, statements like, "I am going to office every day." In Tagalog, there is only one form for the present and the progressive form of the verb. Hence, one says, *"Pumapasok ako araw-araw* (I go to office every day)" or *"Pumapasok na ako ngayon* (I go to school now)."

135

Different Usage of Certain English Words

Dumaan (often translated "pass") and its various forms, depending on the tense, is a very versatile Tagalog word and means "to go by," "to pass by," "to pick up," "to stop for," "to go." Thus a Filipino tends to use the word "pass" in situations where an English-speaking Westerner won't. Note the following examples:

1. "I'll pass for you at seven." *Dadaanan kita sa alas siyete.* I'll pick you up at seven.
2. "I'll pass Hong Kong." *Dadaan ako sa Hong Kong.* I'll go via Hong Kong.
3. "I'll pass by the library and borrow a book." *Dadaan ako sa aklatan at manghihiram ako ng libro.* I'll stop by the library and borrow a book.

Another Tagalog word that is used in various situations and its various forms is *bumaba* ("to go down.") It is used to refer to getting off a bus, getting out of a cab, going down the stairs or going down from any high place. That is why a Westerner hears the following:

1. "He got down the cab in a hurry." *Nagmamadali siyang bumaba sa kab.* He got out of the cab in a hurry.
2. "How can we go down this bus?" *Paano tayo bababa sa bus na ito?* How can we get off this bus?
3. "Stop here. I'm going down already." *Para na dito. Bababa na ako.* Stop here. I'm getting off.

When Filipinos say they "slept late" they generally mean that they stayed up late. It may be a more logical way of expressing the fact that they went to bed in the wee hours of the morning. *Sleeping late* means sleeping till late or waking up late, and not a delayed bedtime. For the English-speaking Westerner the correct phrase for going to bed late is *staying up late*.

Tagalog Idioms Translated into English

Sometimes the "strangeness" of Filipino English comes from the fact that the Filipino is translating a Tagalog idiom into

136

English word for word.

A Filipino wanting to compliment a well-dressed Westerner or American friend says that the Westerner or American "was ready for his funeral" (*nakapamburol*, "dressed for his funeral"). The Westerner or American couldn't understand that the Filipino was saying that he was "dressed to kill."

A Filipino who is not particularly impressed with an office-mate who has been given a promotion attributes the other person's success to his having "oiled" (*nilangisan*) his employer, i.e., "buttered him up."

Asked what the time is, the Filipino apologetically replies that "his watch is dead" or *patay ang relos*, i.e., "his watch has stopped."

A Filipino would ask his Westerner friend to "open the light" (*buksan mo ang ilaw*) meaning, "put on the light."

Social Amenities in English and Tagalog

Certain social formulas in English and Tagalog when taken literally lead to misunderstanding.

For instance, a Filipino woman couldn't understand why an American who promised to see her never did so. It was only after it was explained to her that "I'll see you" is an expression of leave-taking equivalent to the Tagalog *"Diyan ka na"* (literally, "You be there," i.e., Goodbye) that she was consoled. The American didn't break a promise after all!

Likewise, a Westerner may not be aware that such "nosey" questions as *Saan ka pupunta?* "Where are you going?" are simply greetings equivalent to the English "Hi!" or "Hello."

A female Westerner who is complemented by a Filipino as "homely" (meaning "ugly" for English-speaking people) should not feel insulted. The Filipino simply means that she is very much dedicated to her family and usually stays at home.

Filipino Behavior in His Speech

There is a certain "strange" Filipino behavior which is closely tied up with his speech. This comes from the differences between the structures and idioms of the English and the

137

Filipino languages.

A Westerner, for example, couldn't understand why a Filipino said that he would try to meet the Westerner although he had no intention of doing so. He simply did not think it right to say he couldn't make it. He thought he'd save his Western friend's feelings that way. The Filipino didn't know that he had annoyed the Westerner not only because he had made him waste precious time waiting for him but also because he was not true to his word.

When the Filipino says "I'll try to come," it usually means one of three things:

1. I can't come but I don't want to hurt your feelings by saying "No."
2. I'd like to, but I'm not sure you really want me to come. Please insist that I do.
3. I'll probably meet you but I'll not say "yes." Something might prevent me from coming.

A Westerner who asks a Filipino, "How about having dinner with me tonight? I'll pick you up at seven," means that he wants to have the Filipino for dinner at seven.

And the American expects him to say "Fine, I'll see you at seven," or "I can't make it tonight. How about tomorrow night?" That the Westerner invites "casually" does not mean that he is not sincere about his invitation. And he expects a direct answer.

The Filipino, who feels uncomfortable about accepting what seems a casual invitation, unless it is repeated, gives the impression that he is not interested. If the Westerner is "wise," he will ask his Filipino friend a second or third time and the Filipino will agree "reluctantly."

A Filipino who wants a friend for dinner usually gives a "strong" invitation to distinguish it from the *pabalat bunga* (literally, "skin of the fruit," i.e., insincere, casual) invitation. A casual invitation is also described as "coming from the nose" —*sa ilong nanggagaling* (meaning "not from the heart").

The Filipino "Yes"

Foreigners and critics of Filipino behavior are oftentimes

baffled by a positive answer to an appointment or to instructions given only to discover later on that the same individual did exactly the opposite—without cancelling the appointment or asking questions regarding the clarity of the instructions. An average Filipino will say "yes" when:

1. He does not know.
2. He wants to impress.
3. He is annoyed.
4. He wants to end the conversation.
5. He half-understands the instruction or what is being said.
6. He is not sure of himself.
7. He thinks he knows better than the one speaking to him.

Usually the Filipino agrees weakly instead of giving a flat refusal of "No." *Siguro nga, Marahil, Pipilitin ko* ("Maybe," "Perhaps," or "I'll try") are his usual answers to questions to which a Westerner would really say "No." This is because of the Filipino desire to please in spite of the negative response. To interpret the meaning of this "I'll try" or such similar vague answers, requires only a little persuasion to change the vague "I'll try" to a reluctant "yes" or an apologetic "no."

The Filipino's reluctance to refuse or disagree directly is carried over in discussions. One who differs with a speaker feels that he should not appear to do so. He handles this by saying, "Correct me if I am wrong" or "This is not a criticism, I simply want to clarify certain points," "In my own personal opinion . . .," as an introduction to what he really wants to say.

Sex in Speech

For Filipinos topics related to sex are not discussed openly. They should be talked about with refinement and only indirectly. The words "pregnancy" and "pregnant" are generally avoided in favor of the non-formal ways of expressing that condition: "on the way" and "expecting." It is much better English to use the formal words, but many Filipinos believe that they are not polite.

"Conceiving" is used by many Filipinos to mean the early part of pregnancy and its attendant discomforts. They will say, for instance, with a straight face and no hint of malice, "My wife could not come because she is conceiving." Since the moment of conception usually occurs in extremely intimate circumstances and with a partner, such an announcement is liable to raise a few eyebrows at least.

Another example is the phrase "making love." For the Westerner the phrase means the sexual act. For most Filipinos "making love" is believed to be no more harmless than "courting," or "wooing." A Filipino once spoke of a mutual friend to a Westerner: "I am a very good friend of her husband. I was their constant companion when he was making love to her."

Whereupon the poor Westerner spluttered over his drink and had to be slapped several times on his back to restore his breathing to normal. But it was not till after that linguistic quaintness had been explained that he became quite sure he had not strayed into bad company.

Filipino parents do not talk about or name the sexual organs in front of their children. The male sex organ is referred to as "bird" and the female sex organ, as "flower." In most Filipino homes, the subject of sex is taboo and cannot be raised over the dinner table.

Circumlocutions and Polite Indirections

Filipinos are very fond of circumlocutions and polite indirections when they are dealing with foreigners and people of higher strata. A form of circumlocution or at least of polite indirection manifested in their speech is the constant use of the progressive form. An example is "I am inviting you to a banquet next month," in which the invitation is expressed in a state of continuing progress for a long time rather than as an explicit quickly completed action. Or, "I am wishing that you will come," instead of "wish you'd come."

The use of the progressive form among Filipinos is probably due to the fact that it is the very form most often used in Tagalog or Pilipino. "The King is inviting you" is only the Tagalog or Pilipino way of saying "The King cordially invites you."

Most Filipinos are euphemistic. They choose to give opinions in as pleasant words as possible and avoid using harsh and insulting words. This trait is of high value in Philippine society.

To say "stupid" or "crazy" to a Filipino who commits a mistake would cause immediate resentment. In order to preserve harmony and good feelings between the Westerner and the Filipino, it would be advisable for the former to tone down his voice in speaking to the latter. Among Westerners, negative remarks and anger can be expressed loudly and vociferously and usually no harm is done; often results are quick and forthcoming when one displays a show of righteous indignation. Among Filipinos, it is a different story. Speaking in a raised voice, shouting, swearing and showing violent displays of temper are considered inexcusable. The Filipino involved will suffer a loss of face (*mapapahiya*), and the Westerner who has shown anger will suffer a loss of respect that he may never regain.

Comments on a Filipino or his work should be given in a round-about way. The Filipino feels that he and his work are one. Criticism of his work becomes a criticism of himself as a person. Thus he reacts to criticisms emotionally unless they are couched in a language that is not hurtful, that considers his feelings.

The critic is expected to say that he feels he is not qualified to make the comments but since he has been asked to, he will try his best to contribute to the discussion. The person whose work is being discussed answers that he welcomes any suggestions and that he feels that the other person is most qualified to improve on his work. This verbal exchange can be annoying to the Westerner, who may feel it a waste of time to trade compliments. Why not get down to brass tacks?

In this situation, the motivation for the euphemism is not only the desire to please and to get along, but also the reluctance to embarrass (*hiyain*) the other person.

Asking Questions or Not Asking Them at All

While the Filipino round-about way of saying things can be annoying to the Westerner, the Filipino tendency to ask direct questions which the Westerner considers personal can be upsetting. Such "nosey" questions as "Are you married?," "How much do you make a month?," etc. are meant to show one's concern for the other person. It is all part of *pakikisama* or "getting along well." In fact, if an unpleasant encounter cannot

141

be helped—say, if a manager has to call down his subordinate or if a principal has to scold a teacher—one of the indications that an attempt is being made to lessen the hurt or minimize the unpleasantness is in this showing of concern for the person's private life. Thus, after a manager has told his subordinate to work harder because office efficiency suffers because of him, he abruptly switches to an "And how are your wife and children?" routine. This relieves the employee and makes him feel that he still belongs, that he is still accepted. Otherwise, he resents the criticism and does not accept it. The person criticized concludes that the manager is unmindful of other people's feelings and is difficult to get along with.

But although prone to ask "nosey" questions, there is a reluctance on the part of a Filipino to ask questions in situations where a Westerner ordinarily will. American Fulbrighters who have taught in the Philippines often wonder why they usually get a respectful silence when they expect their Filipino students to react to certain issues they bring up in class.

One possible explanation for this is the Filipino attitude towards his teachers and professors. Since they are considered the epitome of wisdom, it is unthinkable for most students to question them. Besides, some Filipino professors do not encourage questions and consider their positions being challenged when students do so. In order to "get along" with such professors, students usually keep quiet and refrain from openly disagreeing with them.

Another possible reason why the Filipino refuses to ask questions is that it is "shameful," *nakakahiya*, to do so. There is a popular belief that only the stupid and the ignorant and the *provinciano* (here used to mean "from the backwoods") ask questions. A Filipino, for instance, would rather get lost looking for an address than ask for directions. A maid would rather pretend to understand the instructions given her and risk making a mistake than ask questions.

The Filipino way of asking for information is to be apologetic about it. One should say something like "Excuse me. May I ask a question?" literally, "May I lose my courtesy? Is it possible to ask?"). After the information has been given, one should apologize for having been a bother.

In the Philippines, one should not barge in on someone and ask a Filipino to do something for him. "Are you busy?" or

"May I disturb you?" are the necessary preludes to what one wants to say. And even if one is busy, he doesn't say so and makes the other person feel that he has all the time for him. "*Basta ikaw*, all the time" (anything for you), he would say.

Hiya is most noticeable in dealings between superiors and subordinates. Usually, a subordinate who calls on a superior specifically to ask for a favor doesn't find the courage to do so until he is almost ready to leave. Then he makes it appear that the favor he is asking is only an afterthought. So he says something like: "Incidentally, I wonder if you can lend me some pesos for my sick child."

The perfect superior makes it easy for the caller to ask for a favor by asking him what he can do for him. And when the subordinate hesitates, he insists that he tells him with admonition not to be shy (*Huwag na kayong mahiya*, often translated "Don't be ashamed").

Even in courtship, a spurned suitor is told graciously that it is not because he has undesirable qualities that the girl can't marry him. It's simply because the girl feels she's "too young to think of marriage," *wala pa sa loob ko* (literally, "not within me yet," i.e., "I haven't given it a thought"). She insists that they remain good friends so that he will not lose face.

At dances, a girl has to be careful about refusing to dance with a boy she does not like. Such an excuse as "I'm tired" or "I don't know how" must be substantiated, i.e., the girl must be careful to sit out that particular dance. Otherwise, it gives the "humiliated" man what he considers a legitimate excuse to create trouble.

The Expatriate Boss and the Filipino Subordinates

Let us take a look at the case of Westerners who come to the Philippines assigned as executives in business establishments. The Filipino sees the Westerner as bigger, richer, more articulate and speaks English fluently. The Filipino sees himself as inferior because he is short, poor and doesn't speak English well. The Westerner in turn does feel superior. Usually in situations where he has the upper hand because of economic and political factors, he begins to see himself as basically superior kind of human being. In this relationship, each party's perceptions are reinforced

143

by the other. As a consequence of this type of relationship, there are two alternative courses of action for the Westerner. One is to stick to his exclusive villages for the rich in Makati and membership in his exclusive clubs. Anyway he has very little to do socially with Filipinos because he feels he has little to gain from this relationship.

The other possible course of action is to have a feeling that it is his responsibility to help the less fortunate Filipinos. He believes that he should show the Filipinos what is the true, the good, and the beautiful—bring to them the good life. Unfortunately this idea of the good life is what he left behind in the good old Western World; and therefore he attempts to transplant various aspects of this life on Philippine soil as a gesture of good-will.

This symptom of superiority complex is very prevalent in the business world. Expatriates are taken in by multinational companies to be appointed as managers in the Philippines. They usually come from the mother plant or company from the base country. Many multinational companies have "imported" foreigners to be placed in top level management for varied reasons, among which are the following:

1. To protect the mother company's investment;
2. To train Filipino managers for eventual appointment to top level positions;
3. They do not trust the Filipino managers to be as "competent" as they.

What then is the relationship of expatriate bosses to the Filipino subordinates especially with regard to the values of "hiya" and "pakikisama?" Because of "hiya" (shyness) Filipinos have the tendency to hold back whatever they want to do for fear of being embarrassed. Even just in talking to these foreigners, Filipinos have the tendency to act in shyness. This is particularly true when the Filipino concerned has a middle level income and education. Even if the Filipinos have bright ideas, they have the tendency to hold back their thoughts before their foreign bosses. Because of their shyness and bashfulness, the Filipino subordinate cannot express what he really wants. He might try to demand for a raise, but cannot express so. Or he may be angry at his foreigner-boss, but cannot tell him so.

144

Take the case of an expatriate who scolds his Filipino subordinate because the latter cannot fully comprehend a technical process. The Filipino subordinate will be surely "mapapahiya" (put into a shameful situation) with his circle of friends. Furthermore the expatriate can say a lot of other things (even if it is with good intentions) which can cause undue embarrassment. This will definitely cause a gap between the Filipino subordinate and his Western boss. Consequently this becomes a detriment to harmonious working and productivity. Furthermore, when intense conflict is induced, there might even be sabotage of each other's performance—back-talking or physical injury.

Often times, Western bosses are perceived by Filipino subordinates as brutally frank, opportunistic, insincere, exploitative or at best, patronizing, awkward and naive. The Western boss, on the other hand, is hurt and defensive and turns to justifying his every action.

For the Filipino subordinate, it is difficult to communicate with his Western boss who is unquestioningly adored or hated. It is impossible to establish constructive relationship and bonds with someone patronized or feared. Furthermore, Western bosses could answer questions about their professional expertise but are tongue-tied when questions are directed to their person—their motives, desires, strengths and weaknesses. To a Filipino, this comes as a surprise because he has regarded a Westerner as an assertive man. A Filipino perceives a Westerner as a frank individual who says what he wants and sometimes is inconsiderate of people's feelings. How come that he becomes tongue-tied to such questions? The Filipino then becomes aware of ulterior motives in the relationship.

Though some expatriates expect others to be as candid and as open as they are, some Western bosses who have stayed long in the Philippines prefer submissive and nonassertive employees. These Western executives get irked when their frankness is matched by their Filipino subordinates.

Multinationals in the Philippines

Some multinational companies fail in the Philippines, not necessarily because of marketing or production difficulties but because of managerial incompetence. In a situation where labor appears cheap and profits quite easy there is a strong tendency to underestimate the importance of good management. Multinational companies usually send experienced people to run their branches in developed European countries, but often send people with no visible qualifications to smaller and underdeveloped countries. They forget that in the Philippines, though the economic growth is not as significant as in the developed countries, the people have educational qualifications as significant as in any developed country. And since local labor is very cheap but management (imported) expensive, there is the tendency to use *little management* and *much labor.* Unaware of cultural factors, the production operations in the Philippine branch or plant are usually engineered much the same way as in the head office or main plant.

Consequently, management does little or nothing at all to adjust to the culture of the people. The general attitude is that there are general principles—of course those held in the mother country. Thus they bring in to the local scene the mother company policy, systems, philosophy, and technology. The "culture-bound theory" considers that what a manager does is very widely affected by culture in a direct way, and that such effects can be as important as type of work or company size. This theory sees culture as modifying the situation at all levels. It affects the contextual and structural level through the organizational principles and business practices, and through the preferences and "philosophies" of those responsible for structuring the organization. The formation of roles is affected by the orientation of managers towards concepts such as authority, control, definition, work. The actual behavior in the organization is partly governed by the members' interpretation of socially acceptable behavior in organizations and relations with others.

Take the case of workers recruited from agricultural provinces. These workers were born and nurtured in a *gemeinschaft* culture, a type of community life in which intimate, sympathetic and neighborly relationships prevail. There has been considerable speculation about the adjustments involved in shifting from agricultural work in the country to urban living and factory discipline where the gesellschaft culture prevails. This is now another environment and type of community life in which impersonal, superficial, and business-like relationships prevail. How severely do workers resent the constraints placed on them by machine pacing, close supervision, and the need for regular attendance at work? How long does it take them to adapt the attitudes and behavior patterns of mature industrial workers? Organizational principles in this situation should be viewed by management in the actual company context. Where such principles require structures, roles, and behavior which are not compatible with the cultural orientations and concepts of acceptable social conduct held by members of an organization, there is bound to be trouble.

There are certain effects of cultural traditions on Filipino worker behavior. There is a strong tradition of personal dependence on the head of the enterprise. Filipino factory workers appear to court paternalism instead of resenting it. There is a cultural resistance to women working and earning high incomes in a traditionally male-dominated society. There is a strong jealousy on the part of the senior workers to see a younger worker receiving higher salary in spite of higher expertise. Traditions of family responsibility and hospitality sometimes conflict with regular attendance at work.

Western managers tend to underestimate the rationality, economic motivation, and potential productivity of their Filipino workers. The above-mentioned cultural carryovers are not insurmountable to effect high productivity. All facets of the company philosophy, principles, and operating systems, however, should be checked for cultural fit. Western managers should realize that the cultural or cross-cultural area is of prime importance for all stages of management; furthermore, the Western-style systems should be carefully vetted and adapted to the local situation and culture.

Another serious area of stress is the difference in the way Filipinos and Westerners come to understand a situation. When a Westerner is talking to somebody, he listens to *what* the person is saying, to the *content* of his speech. To the Filipino, this is less important. When he listens to a person, his immediate instinctive reaction is to try and figure out what the speaker is like, what kind of a person he is; and by identifying with the speaker, he can better understand what he is talking about. An understanding process which relies on "objective" data and one which makes use of identification with the persons involved often can arrive at different interpretations of the same situation. The Westerner does not know that if the Filipino cannot identify who he is, neither does he believe the Westerner's words even if objectively he is right.

The Transplant Syndrome

The transplant syndrome is a phenomenon where the values and aspirations of those governing, strategized by their unique managerial processes, eventually become the norms of thought and behavior of the governed. This is a phenomenon shared by those governing and the governed culture over time.

This transplant syndrome is pervasive among Westerners who come to the Philippines as managers and executives, who transplant sometimes lock-stock-and-barrel the planning formats and managerial systems of highly advanced Western societies, rather than develop a model rooted to the Filipino environment, compatible with the Filipino context, and in harmony with Filipino values.

The expatriate must have in mind that the Filipino has his own peculiar concerns, aspirations and values. Thus, transplanting a foreign model without experiencing the process of its conceptualization and birth results into a mixture that is often a hodge-podge of style of unsubstantial imitation. To implement a purely Japanese management style in the Philippines for the Filipinos will be ineffective. To sell or market a product in the Philippines, the American way may be ineffective.

A well known marketing man, Herb Liss, served as advertising manager of Proctor and Gamble in the Philippines for a few years before he was reassigned to other countries. He returned a few years later and made a very interesting observation. He said he had launched a new product in South America which was a tremendous success. From there he was transferred to Spain where he launched the same product with an even more resounding success. So he was sent to the Philippines to do the same. It was a flop. He could not understand why. This is proof that the Filipino is unique. His values, idiosyncracies and motivations are different from those of other countries.

148

Filipino Humor

Laughter spices the life of the Filipino. Without it, life for him becomes a mere routine and brings about sheer boredom.

To a foreigner, the friendly smile of the Filipinos seen among people in the barrios, in the cities, in fact anywhere, is a calling card—one that easily wins friends and makes expatriates feel that they are welcome to this country. That smile brings along undertones of gallantry, generosity and hospitality. Besides smiling when they are happy, Filipinos also smile when they feel shy or are embarrassed.

Laughter, to the Filipinos, can be a kind of psychological therapy in time of difficulties, problems and untoward incidents. For example, when people inside a public bus are perspiring, overcrowded and anxious because of the heavy traffic, it is enough for just one passenger to crack a joke like, "So this is how sardines in a can feel," referring to the fully packed bus, and the whole atmosphere is changed from one of tension and anxiety into one of laughter and joy. Filipinos are said to be one rare breed of people who can laugh even at themselves.

One thing worth noting, however, is the fact that Filipinos and Westerners do not laugh at the same things. Sometimes the Westerner finds it hard to understand why a Filipino and his Filipino friends are rolling in laughter only to find that the joke or the humor in a particular situation simply cannot be explained. Aside from the language problem, the Filipinos have a different sense of the humorous. Filipinos have a much easier time laughing at themselves than Westerners do. Laughing at himself is one of the more important coping mechanisms of the Filipino. Sometimes playful, sometimes cynical, he manages to laugh even at times when the Westerner would consider laughter inappropriate. Westerners can also be perplexed by the apparent sadism in Filipino humor. This is particularly true in teasing, where a person can be teased relentlessly with neither the person teased nor the teasers seeming to tire of what may seem to an outsider as a senselessly repetitious activity. To the Filipino involved in the teasing, this is a means of letting off steam, of socializing and of showing affection. Because Filipinos and Westerners laugh at different things they sometimes have difficulty feeling comfortable with each other.

The Filipino Sociostat

Sociostat is a popular conversational technique which regulates social behavior. One way it operates is to cut down to size any individual who publicly takes credit for an act or claims any kind of superiority over his in-group.

Thus, a Westerner who has just returned from studies abroad and is eagerly telling his friends in the Philippines how hard a course he took was, but how he passed it anyway, may get the subtle response, "How much did you pay your professor to get your good grades?"

If a Filipino does not go around with his peers as much as he used to before he stayed in Europe/America he is likely to hear remarks like, "It must be so hard for you to readjust to life in the Philippines, now that you are already an American/European!"

Westerners consider traits like assertiveness, pride, aggressiveness, frankness and familiarity as assets to a person. In the Philippines, however, virtues of politeness, humility, modesty and passiveness are more greatly admired in a person. One is expected to be modest in speech and not boastful. If a Filipino notices one's new shirt and says, "You have a very beautiful shirt. I'm sure that is very expensive."

The owner is expected to answer, "Oh, this is very *cheap*. I bought it from an ordinary store." This he says although the shirt is really expensive. On the other hand, when one asks another, "Does my shirt look so ugly?" the one asked is expected to answer, "No, it looks very good on you." The sociostat must work to maintain smooth interpersonal relationships. This is known as the *levelling technique* which runs: "If a Filipino exalts you, you should humble yourself; if he humbles himself, he expects you to exalt him."

The technique of levelling a person is reinforced by the indirect method of criticism known as gossip. Anything out of the ordinary becomes the topic of conversation of the week, especially in the small community. The winner in the sweepstakes, for example, who does not give the traditional "blowout" is talked about disparagingly and he is made to know about it. Through a system of intermediaries popularly known as the grapevine, the deviant is made painfully aware of his shortcomings in the eyes of his in-group. He usually does something about it to maintain his good social standing.

150

The Kaleidescopic Character of the Filipino

If a Westerner were to observe the true character of the Filipinos—how they feel, how they think, and how they react to different situations—one way is to go to two of the oldest Filipino institutions: the cockpit and the market place.

Cockfighting existed even before Ferdinand Magellan came to the Philippines. The market has been a traditional place and source of news which, up to the present, is a sound barometer of the economic condition of the Philippines. In the cockpit, the Filipino can be seen at his very worst and at his very best. At his very worst, the Filipino is neckdeep in vice; in his famous *bahala na* (literally, it means "let it be") attitude, he can take his entire harvest, the family savings, and the money for food and clothing to bet on a single *sultada*. At his very best, the honest Filipino, during a cockfight, pays his account to the last centavo. The trustful Filipino bets against the first person he sees without questioning his integrity and capacity to pay; he is the good sport who takes his heavy losses good-naturedly.

Abroad, some Filipino seamen have created an image of the Filipino as a quarrelsome breed who tends to gang up with others of his country to fight it out with any other ethnic group willing to take them on. In general, this is not so. The Filipinos are a peace-loving people. They can easily accept as friends and brothers nationals of other countries, both from the East and the West.

The first known migrants to the country were the Negritos (little black people as the Spaniards called them) and the Agtas (Aetas). The Agtas are black-skinned and kinky-haired pygmies who came in dugouts 25,000 years ago. Following them were descendants of the different people who migrated to the country thereafter: the tall Indonesians of the Mongoloid race, the Malayans, Proto-Malays, Borneans, and other types of Malayans, followed by Chinese, Indian, Arab, Japanese, Spanish, British, and the Americans. The Filipinos have imbibed both oriental and occidental ways.

Duane Quintal, one of the world's most successful industrial designers, has designed many famous products for many countries. His product designs are everyday words in the Philippines: Vitalis, Finch Paints, Colgate, Scott Paper, Sanitex, Tender Care, to mention but a few. Mr. Quintal says that the Philippines is the

151

most unusual country he has ever worked in. He claims that
if a product were launched in the Philippines with remarkable
success that product will be accepted almost anywhere in the
world. He says that more and more people from other countries
are beginning to recognize the Philippines as an ideal test market
because of the international characteristics and culture of the
Filipinos.

"Stateside" Mentality of the Filipino

The Filipino way of thinking that everything foreign is good
still remains embedded in his personality. The distrust for anything made locally is still with him. This explains the preference
that the Filipino has for European or "Stateside" goods. He has a
propensity for imported goods and easily adapts to foreign ideas
and ways. The true, the good, and the beautiful to the Filipino is
what looks Greek, Semitic, or generally Caucasian. It is in this
regard that the Filipino is different from other Orientals. The
Japanese patronize their products, even if these are inferior compared to the foreign-made ones. The Indian sticks to his Indian
ways and ideas. The Filipino prefers the foreign ones. For him
soap made with olive oil is superior to soap made with local
coconut oil. The basic feeling behind such judgment may be a
relic of centuries of colonial rule when the mother country was
looked up to as the source of superior goods and a superior way
of life. Long after the objective need is gone, one continues to
depend upon the symbolic parental figure.

11 ENJOYING LIFE IN THE PHILIPPINES

The Philippines—the "Pearl of the Orient," "the Crossroads of the Pacific," and "the only Christian nation in the Far East,"—has always been an attraction to the civilized eyes of cultured Europeans and monied Americans.

The Filipino people and its islands are naturally hospitable and open to coming foreigners offering them the best that they can offer. Every type of foreigner can find a cozy place in the Philippines. Manila alone has 10,000 first class hotel rooms available. This is the center of government, business and culture. The city is linked to the various world capitals via radio, cable and microwave communication. Radio, telephone and telegraph systems connect the different towns and cities in the country. Manila can offer one the best educational institutions in the Orient, art galleries, museums, historic old churches as well as theaters, discos, nightclubs and discotheques.

Filipinos are also good cooks. Philippine cuisine is a blend of Malay, Chinese, and Spanish influences. Native cuisines are exotic. American food and restaurants also abound.

The country offers a variety of scenic places for foreigners to visit during weekends and long summer and Christmas vacations. Some of them are Baguio, the summer capital; the Taal Volcano of Tagaytay City; the beaches of Cebu, Mindoro, Palawan; the Chocolate Hills of Bohol and Zamboanga, the "City of Flowers," and Pagsanjan Falls in Laguna.

Transportation is no problem. Manila is connected by daily flights to the major cities of the world. Within the Philippines the Philippine Airlines has regular scheduled flights to all the cities throughout the country. Land transportation facilities in Manila and in the provinces are abundant. Buses, taxicabs and jeepneys are the usual means of transportation in the country. There are air-conditioned buses available, too. The Philippine National Railways services the island of Luzon, reaching as far north as San Fernando, La Union and as far south as Legaspi City in Albay.

Festivals

One thing expatriates enjoy very much in the Philippines are the festivals. For Filipinos, there is always cause for celebration. To give thanks for a good harvest, to honor a saint, to commemorate a victory, to renew a pact of friendship. Thus, patron saints, mythical figures, historical events are all invoked for the purpose of holding a festival. These festivals are always colorful, sometimes grandiose, always fun. With typical exuberance, they will throw open their homes, invite friends, relations and total strangers to sit down and partake of a feast. For the Filipino believes in sharing what he has, and a *fiesta* is the best excuse for expressing his extravagant nature. It is only natural, then, that his calendar would be filled with festivals, for life after all, should be a feast. Among the festivals are the following:

New Year's Day — January is National Holiday
Next only to Christmas, the New Year celebration is the most anticipated festivity by the Filipinos. It is customary for Filipino families to be together on New Year's eve. The highlights of the celebration are a colorful spectacle of fireworks, noise and merry making followed by *media noche* or midnight repast. Catholics end the celebration by attending an early morning mass.

Feast of the Three Kings — 1st Sunday of January
Celebration of the final phase of the Yuletide gift-giving and the various celebrations of the Christmas season. In the towns of Sta. Cruz and Gasan, Marinduque, people gather in a colorful procession re-enacting the journey of the Three Wise Men.

Feast of the Black Nazarene — January 9, Quiapo, Manila
Bare-footed Christian male devotees, towels around their necks, carry the centuries-old image of the Black Nazarene

154

through the winding streets of Quiapo in an afternoon procession. There is a mammoth mass of men elbowing and pushing their way towards the statue of the Black Christ, for it is believed that whoever carries the palanquin or touches its sacred cargo will be forgiven of sins.

Sto. Niño de Cebu — January 10, Cebu City
This week-long festival, the grandest of Cebu City's fiestas, celebrated in honor of Sto. Niño de Cebu, is marked with the *sinulog* dances, solemn processions, cultural night presentations, fireworks and carnival.

Pipigan — January, Novaliches, Rizal
The festivity revolves around the preparation of pinipig, a native delicacy. Toasted sticky rice is pounded into pinipig to the tune of happy guitar melodies.

Appey — January, Bontoc
Three-day thanksgiving rites for a bountiful harvest.

Mannerway — January, Bontoc
An exotic dance festival to awaken the Bontoc rain gods.

Ati-Atihan — January, Kalibo, Aklan
This mardi-gras style revelry is one of the country's biggest and rowdiest festivals. Kalibo townsfolk, their guests and passersby relive the barter of Panay Island between the aboriginal Atis and the sea-faring Bornean chieftains by painting themselves soot black and uninhibitedly dancing and carousing in the streets for three days.

Feast of Our Lady of Candelaria — February 2, Jaro, Iloilo
The townspeople of Jaro honor their patron saint with religious processions, parades, evening shows, fairs and ceremonies that bear the rich variety of the Ilongo's cultural heritage.

Chinese New Year — February 16, Chinatown
The Chinese in the Philippines celebrate the new Lunar Year with their Filipino neighbors and friends. Festivities include the Dragon Dance weaving through the streets of Chinatown in Manila, open-air Chinese operas and plays, feasting and merry-making.

155

Hari Raya Hadji — February, Muslim Provinces
Holiday marking the Muslims' annual pilgrimage to Mecca.

Tinagba — February 11, Iriga City
Harvest festival highlighted by a colorful parade of carts laden with the best local produce.

Feast of Our Lady of Lourdes — February 11, Quezon City
The feast is held to commemorate the Lady of Lourdes' apparition in Lourdes, France. Masses and processions are held specially in the centers of celebrations—the Shrine of the Virgin in Lourdes Church in Quezon City and the Grotto in Novaliches, Rizal.

Valentine's Day — February 14
Sweethearts, lovers and friends celebrate their day.

Bale Zamboanga Festival — February 24-25, Zamboanga City
Cultural shows, fairs, regattas and religious services are participated in by Christians and Muslims alike.

Saranggolahan — March, Luzon Region
A prelude to the summer season celebrated by kite flying contests.

Baguio Summer Festival — March, Baguio City
Baguio City, the Philippines' summer capital, plays host for the country's summer fiesta; a whole week of celebration—music, sports, parades, ethnic displays and contests.

Iloilo Regatta — March, Iloilo City
The sea dotted with racing *paraws* (native sailboats) is one of Iloilo City's summer spectacles.

Araw ng Davao — March 10-16, Davao City
A six-day festivity to mark Davao City's foundation. The festival features religious processions, civic-military parades and cultural fairs—with ethnic exhibits, carnivals and beauty queens.

Moriones Festival — March, Marinduque
This is a festivity which dramatizes the Passion of Jesus

156

Christ and the beheading of Longinus, a one-eyed Roman Centurion who submitted himself to the Christian faith after his defective eye had been cured by a drop of blood that his own lance had squirted out of Christ's body. It is called "Moriones" because the Marinduque folk art version of Roman centurions are the masked morions.

Palm Sunday — March or April

Filipino Christians waving fronds of palm leaves proceed to their churches to be blessed as symbols of Christ's triumphant entry to Jerusalem. This event ushers in the Holy Week.

Holy Week — March or April

For seven days the Christian Filipinos solemnly participate in the observance of the Passion of Christ. Flagellants on the streets, processions and *Senakulos* (passion plays), are part of the Lenten observance one is bound to encounter almost anywhere in the islands. The most solemn of all religious festivals occurs on *Good Friday* (a public holiday) when Christians commemorate the crucifixion of Christ while the most glorious celebration is on *Easter Sunday* when the Christian world rejoices at the Resurrection.

Sinulog Festival — March 25, Ilog, Negros Occidental

The celebration centers around the Negros townsfolk's rendition of an exotic tribal dance called "sinulog." One of the two dances still preserved by Mundos, primitive tribe of Indonesian origin, "Sinulog" was choreographed centuries ago around the tribe's fertility rites. Essentially, this unique dance festival is a marriage of religion and folklore.

Feast of Virgen de Turumba — April, Pakil, Laguna

Devotees jump, fall, leap or dance with joy as they follow the image of Our Lady of Sorrows in procession. "Turumba" is a corruption of the Tagalog word *tumumba* meaning to fall.

Bataan Day — April 9

Today's Filipino remembers and salutes the bravery of the fighters who defended the island during World War II. On Bataan Day both Filipinos and foreigners visit the Mt. Samat Shrine and *Dambana ng Kagitingan* (Altar of Courage).

Handugan — 4th Week of April, San Jose, Antique

The landing of the ten Bornean datus in Panay Island before the Spaniards came is celebrated in Antique with riotous dancing and singing in the streets. Antiqueños blacken themselves with soot and dress up in imitation of the aborigines.

Magellan's Landing — April 24, Cebu City

A festive commemoration of Ferdinand Magellan's historic landing in Cebu in 1521, when the Philippine Archipelago was discovered for the Western World. Cebuanos re-enact the event replete with a fluvial parade, contests, plays and the authentic Magellan Cross.

Labor Day — May 1, National Holiday

A national holiday to honor the Filipino workers.

Santacruzan — May 1-30

A much-cherished Filipino tradition, this Maytime festival is highlighted by a procession and pageant that recalls the quest of Queen Helena and Prince Constantine for the Holy Cross. The loveliest of the town's women participate in this procession.

Fall of Corregidor — May 6, Corregidor

Military-civic parade and ceremonies are held to commemorate the Battle of Corregidor in 1942. Nostalgia seekers visit Corregidor Island's war relics.

International Sea Fair — May 7-8, Balangit, Bataan

An annual international aquatic sportsfest which includes, among other things, scuba diving and boat races.

Carabao Festival — May 14-15, Pulilan, Bulacan; Nueva Ecija; Angono, Rizal

Hundreds of farmers parade about the church plaza on their well-adorned carabaos to pay their respects to their patron saint, San Isidro Labrador, before commencing a day of games, contests and fun.

Harvest Festival (PAHIYAS) — May 15, Lucban and Sariaya, Quezon

Another colorful celebration to honor the patron saint of the

158

farmers, San Isidro. In an afternoon procession, Quezon townsfolk and their visitors make a mad scramble for fruits and brightly colored Filipino delicacies which hang from windows and
doorways of houses along the route.

Fertility Rites — May 17-19, Obando, Bulacan
    A triple religious fete to honor San Pascual Baylon, Santa
Clara and Virgen de Salambao. Childless couples dance on the
streets to the main altar of the church in the belief that childless
couples who sincerely participate in the fertility dance will be
blessed with a child.

Feast of Our Lady of Peace and Good Voyage — May 1-31, Antipolo, Rizal
    May is the month for pilgrimages to the shrine of the travel-
ler's miraculous patroness, Nuestra Señora de la Paz y Buen Viaje
(patron saint of the Manila-Acapulco Galleon trade) in the town
of Antipolo.

Bulaklakan (Flores de Mayo) — May 1-30
    A month-long celebration held in practically every town and
village to honor the Virgin. The prettiest girls gowned in their
best parade through the streets in candlelit processions that borrow elements from the Bible, history, mythology and the Filipino's rich imagination.

Pista ng Krus — June, Obando, Bulacan
    A fluvial procession for a bountiful harvest is held.

Philippine Independence Day — June 12, National Holiday
    A mammoth military-civic parade at the Rizal Park marks the
commemoration of the first Philippine Independence Day when
Gen. Emilio Aguinaldo proclaimed independence from Spanish
rule in 1896.

Lechon Parade — June 24, Balayan, Batangas
    An extremely festive parade of golden-brown, crispy "le-
chon" (roast pig) is the Batangueños' way of honoring St. John
the Baptist.

Feast of St. John the Baptist — June 24, San Juan, Rizal

Residents douse friends and passers-by (in good humor), to celebrate the Baptism of Christ, by St. John in the River Jordan. The day also marks the celebration of the San Juan fiesta.

Halaran Festival — June 24, Roxas City, Capiz

A gay festivity surrounds the re-enactment of the purchase of Panay Island by the Bornean datus with riotous tribal fancy parades.

Our Lady of Perpetual Help — June 27, Baclaran, Rizal

A major religious procession and mass is celebrated by the Catholic devotees in the spirit of the Wednesday novenas at the Baclaran Church.

Saints Peter and Paul — June 28-30, Apalit, Pampanga

A three-day celebration highlighted by a fluvial procession with the images of Saints Peter and Paul along the Apalit River.

Feast of San Pedro — June 29, Davao City

Davao's elegant June fair, it features military-civic parade, carnival, cultural night shows, exhibits and religious procession in honor of San Pedro, Davao City's patron saint.

Bocaue River Festival — 1st Sunday, July, Bocaue, Bulacan

A joyous river festivity, the Holy Cross of Wawa is mounted on an intricately decorated barge and paraded through the Bocaue River escorted by a group of large boats adorned with flowers.

Fil-American Friendship Day — July 4, National Holiday

Formerly the National Independence Day, it is now celebrated as Filipino-American Friendship Day.

Harvest Festival — July 1-30, Mountain Province

The *Tengao Fagfagto* are a combination of pagan and Christian rituals for an abundant crop.

St. Martha River Festival — July 29, Pateros, Rizal

Another river festival, this time in Pateros, Rizal, only twenty minutes ride from Manila: A replica of a crocodile follows the barge that carries the image of St. Martha. Local legend has it

160

that the patroness once miraculously saved the town's duck industry from a dangerous crocodile.

Dance of the Aetas — August 1-7, Bayombong, Nueva Vizcaya
Aetas tribes oin Nueva Vizcaya serenade houses with their exotic tribal dances and songs.

Cry of Balintawak — August 26
National celebration commemorating the beginning of the Filipino revolution against Spain.

Cagayan de Oro City Festival — August 28
Another grand city festival that displays colorful sequences of beauty pageants, military-civic parades and cultural nights.

Sunduan — September 10, La Huerta, Parañaque
The people of Parañaque, Rizal, celebrate one of their treasured traditions. Lovely girls, escorted by young men holding parasols, are fetched from house to house by the town's brass bands.

Peñafrancia Festival — 3rd Weekend of September, Naga City, Camarines Sur
The Blessed Virgin's image is returned to her home shrine via the Naga River in Bicolandia's most spectacular afternoon fluvial procession participated in only by the males. No woman has ever participated in this affair; otherwise, it is believed the procession won't move or the barge will sink.

Ang Sinulog — September 29, Iligan City
Town fiesta in honor of Saint Michael the Archangel. Highlight of the celebration is the *yawa-yawa*, a vernacular play with songs and dances about the life of the glorious warrior-patron Saint Michael.

Davao Tribal Festival — 1st Week of October, Davao City
Highlanders who have their roots in the mountains of Davao Province, perform their tribal dances, songs and traditional rituals in the Davao metropolis—an annual cultural sharing.

Our Lady of Solitude — October 3, Porta Vega, Cavite
Feast of the Blessed Virgin whose image was said to have been found floating on the sea.

Feast of Our Lady of the Pillar — October 12, Zamboanga City
The feast commemorates the Lady's apparition which was said to have taken place at Fort Pilar. The image was discovered there soon after.

La Naval de Manila — 2nd Sunday of October, Sto. Domingo Church, Quezon City
Night procession in honor of the Lady of the Holy Rosary, also known as Virgen dela Naval de Manila. It commemorates the Filipino-Spanish victory over the Dutch marauders in 1646 believed to have been made possible only by the divine intercession of the Virgin.

Landing of the Liberation Allied Forces — October 20, Red Beach, Palo, Leyte
Commemoration of the landing of the World War II Liberation Allied Forces led by Gen. Douglas MacArthur in Red Beach, Leyte.

Pista ng Apo — Last Friday of October, Angeles City, Pampanga
Religious procession in honor of Jesus Christ and the Blessed Virgin Mary. Residents entertain their guests with sumptuous meals.

The Great Sibidan Race — October 21-24, Legaspi City
A sea affair highlighted by "sibidan" (native canoes) race.

Feast of Christ the King — Last Sunday of October
An afternoon all-male procession to honor Christ the King.

All Saints Day — November 1, National Holiday
This is a day for remembering the dead and keeping vigil at the cemeteries.

All Souls Day — November 2
Catholics attend mass and visit churches with the intention of saving the souls in purgatory.

Hariraya Poasa — November, Muslim Provinces

A Muslim festival marking the end of Ramadan, the 30-day fasting period of the Muslim devotees.

Feast of San Clemente — November 23, Angono, Rizal

The main highlight of the San Clemente fiesta is the parade of people bearing paddles and bamboo sticks amidst shouts of "Viva San Clemente!"

Yakan Harvest Festival — November 15-30, Basilan

Thanksgiving feast of Basilan Island's Yakan tribe.

Kaamulan — November 18-20, Malaybalay, Bukidnon

Bukidnon natives perform tribal dances and religious rituals.

Grand Cañao — November 28-December 2, Baguio City

A week of festivities when the tribes of the Mountain Provinces gather in the city to give thanks to their gods through music, dances and rituals.

Feast of Our Lady of the Immaculate Conception — December 8, Roxas City, Capiz; Vigan, Ilocos Sur; Pasig, Metro Manila

Evening processions, cultural presentations, circus, beauty pageants and fireworks are part of this Philippine religious festival in honor of the Immaculate Conception.

Malabon Fluvial Parade — December 8, Malabon, Rizal

Malabon folks honor the Lady of the Immaculate Conception in a massive and colorful parade along the Malabon-Navotas waterway.

Taal Fluvial Festival — December 8-9, Taal, Batangas

Set against the country's twin volcanoes, a rustic fluvial parade highlights the feast of the Blessed Virgin of Casasay.

Pagsanjan Town Fiesta — December 12, Pagsanjan, Laguna

Beautiful bamboo arches are set along the main streets of the town famous for its gorge and rapids.

Simbang Gabi (Midnight Mass) — December 16-25, National Celebration

The longest Christmas in the world is ushered in by a nine-day *novena* in the pre-dawn masses called *Misa de Gallo*, one of the yuletide traditions of the Filipinos.

Panunuluyan — December 24, Regional

Christmas eve re-enactment of the Blessed Virgin's and Saint Joseph's vain search for shelter. In the Visayas, it is called *Panagbalay.*

Lantern Festival — December 24, San Fernando, Pampanga

Christmas eve parade contests of gigantic multi-colored *paroles* (lanterns) with kaleidoscopic designs.

Christmas Day — December 25, National Holiday

This is the celebration of the Nativity.

Bota de Flores — December 26, Ermita, Manila

Floral offerings to the Nuestra Sra. de Guia at the Ermita Church.

Binirayan — December 28-30, San Jose, Antique

The landing of the ten Bornean datus in Panay Island before the Spaniards came is celebrated and reenacted in Antique. Tribes from the mountains come to the towns to join in the celebration.

The Philippine Christmas Season

The Philippines celebrates the longest Christmas season in the world and tradition has had it so for about 200 years. The extension of the *pascuas* to incldue the Feast of the Three Kings is a Spanish tradition. Christmas in the Philippines is a mixture of western and typically Filipino customs and tradition. Among the inherited Christmas customs from the West are the setting up of a Christmas tree, the sending of Christmas cards to loved ones and acquaintances, Santa Claus, the singing of Christmas carols from house to house, the custom of gift-giving, and "Kris Kringle" (the game involving "mystery" mommies or daddies and babies exchanging gifts during the Christmas season). Filipinos sing *Jingle Bells*, *White Christmas*, and *Fa-la-la-la-la-la*, and promote belief in Santa Claus among their children. Santa is the kindly old fat man who rewards good behavior in children with a shower of presents and shows his displeasure by merely omitting a naughty child's name from his gift list. Although Filipino houses (except in Baguio, the summer capital of the Philippines) don't have chimneys through which Santa could enter the house, Filipino parents would reassure their kids that the main door or window would be left ajar. At about eight or nine p.m. of Christmas eve, every child in the house will be brought to bed for a short nap before they are roused from their sleep at about midnight. By that time, Santa would have whisked by and (lo!) left a fortune in gifts in every sock hung by the window or Christmas tree.

The typical Filipino custom during Christmas is the nine-day prelude to Christmas known as *simbang gabi*. Simbang gabi was first held in a certain town in the early 1700s as a thanksgiving mass for a bountiful harvest with the thought of obtaining graces and repeated favors in the coming year.

To make the plan practical, it was further resolved that the novena (9-day prayer) be started exactly nine days before Christmas Day so that the end will coincide with Christmas eve and the feasting that went with *Noche Buena*. This was done with such happy results that the act to obtain graces was repeated the following year, and the next year after that. Soon it spread to neighboring towns and then to the entire countryside.

From this crude beginning evolved the *Misa de Aguinaldo* as Filipino devotees call it, but more popularly called Misa de Gallo. This is because the mass is said at 4 o'clock in the morning, and in some towns even earlier, at cock's crow. The tradition has been preserved and remains an essential element of the Filipinos' Christmas celebration.

Christmas day is the most joyous celebration in every Filipino home. Most homes have the "Belen" or nativity scene alongside the western Christmas tree. Christmas lanterns (paroles) are hung from windows, gaily decorated and brightly lit to add to the festive mood of the season. Christmas for the Filipino is the time for gift-giving, merry-making and the traditional family gatherings. Children go to the houses of relatives, friends and *ninongs* and *ninangs* (godparents) to receive blessings and gifts.

Generally, what Filipinos practice at Christmastime is money exchange. The rule of the game is: Your children's *pamasko* (Christmas gift) for my children's Christmas money. Nephews, nieces, godchildren, grandchildren, and other relatives' children are the usual beneficiaries of the money-giver. A usual Filipino gift on Christmas is a variety of homemade cakes, pies, or pastries. A set of hand-embroidered handkerchiefs or crocheted tablespreads are also gifts given on Christmas.

Various Rites of Filipino Christmas

The Philippines celebrates Christmas in ways as varied as its regions. In the Tagalog regions, especially in Bulacan, there is the *panuluyan* or *panawagan*. It is the part of the Christmas story which commemorates the weary flight of Mary and Joseph when they looked for shelter more than 2000 years ago. It falls on December 16-24. The panuluyan is re-enacted daily before the simbang gabi (midnight mass). A young man and a young girl, representing St. Joseph and Virgin Mary, followed by a string band and the townspeople, sing an appeal for shelter. The owner of the house approached by the panuluyan also sings an excuse that there is "no room" available for them in the house.

In Malolos, Bulacan, the panuluyan is presented only on the night of the 24th, before the *misang pamasko*. It is practical to have a young man and a young woman act out this pastoral pageant complete with dialogue because it comes on live and on the spot. Other towns prefer to present the panuluyan with the use of images of the Blessed Virgin and St. Joseph. At 9:30 in the evening, the panuluyan group, with the townsfolk, moves in procession, usually with the statues of Joseph and Mary in the lead, followed by the church choir, the townspeople and the brass band.

The lantern festival in San Fernando, Pampanga, is among the country's most unique festivals, having been billed as the "most spectacular of its kind in the world." The lanterns of San Fernando are so big that they have to be carried on six-by-six trucks for they measure from 15-30 feet. Each costs from P1,000 to P2,000 or more. On the 24th of December, Christmas eve, a parade and contest of gigantic multi-colored "paroles (lanterns) with kaleidoscopic designs is held.

In Malico, a highland sitio in the Caraballo mountains in Sta. Fe, Nueva Vizcaya, the Kalanguya tribe of Igorots start the Christmas feast in the first week of December when the *Masiken* or their tribal datu summons a palaver to discuss their program of activities. When a program has been finalized, the datu then appoints eight respected members of the clan to help him shoulder the expenses of the activities. In the evening of December 16, the first in a series of celebrations is held in the home of the first of the eight men. Dancing among the younger set and *bakliw* singing among the elders, enliven the drinking of home-brewed *tapuy* (native wine). At midnight, supper is served. Later, they dance and sing until the wee hours.

The merrymaking repeats itself until the eighth man's turn to celebrate. On Christmas eve, the celebration is held at the home of the datu. It is grander and more colorful than the previous affairs. By sundown at least 12 cows would have been skinned and cooked in giant vats. Dancing and bakliw singing start. Meal is served at 8 p.m. and another at midnight. But that does not signal to all a goodnight. For at sunrise breakfast is served. A program follows with speeches and recitations and singing by schoolchildren.

Christmas comes to Aklan, land of the Ati-atihan, with the arrival of folk singers. They come in December in motley groups cradling guitars and goat-skin drums. To the people in the *poblacion*, they sing folk songs depicting the biblical story of the Nativity in the vernacular. Aklan folk songs are long, the lyrics crude and the tune plaintive. During Christmas, the songs are sung by teenage girls who make up the *daigon* or carolers. They are accompanied by elders who strum the guitar and lead the singing. Lighted candles are placed on the doorstep of the serenaded house, adding a touch of the old charms to Christmas in Albay.

In a little-known islet of Anuayan, east of Panay island, the inhabitants have a novel way of celebrating Christmas. The fisherfolk divide their celebration of Christmas into three parts. In the morning of December 24, they hold *parada sa baybayon* (sea parade), participated in by hundreds of fishermen aboard their fishing bancas bedecked with wild flowers and vari-colored paper buntings. Each boat has a *hara* (queen) who showers flowers along the route of the sea parade. This lasts for three hours. In the evening of the same day, the islanders gather together by the sea to hold a pageant depicting the birth of Jesus Christ in a manger in Bethlehem. The participants are dressed in crude but colorful paper costumes prepared weeks before the eve of Christmas. Lanterns and torches add color and spectacle to the dramatic presentation.

These lanterns and torches—hundreds of them—are securely hung or tied to the branches of big trees. The final stage of the activity for Christmas among the people of Anuayan consists of games. These are *dumog* (wrestling), *pukol* (coconut cracking), and the *bulang* (cockfighting). Finally, there is the *punsiyon* (banquet) given in honor of visitors.

Whatever the occasion, a fiesta or festival always offers the best opportunities to make friends with the islanders. For the Filipino is at his best when he is celebrating with friends, and nobody remains a stranger for long.

Manila offers the widest variety of entertainment, with most of the night life centered along Roxas Boulevard and in the Ermita district. Filipinos are born musicians; and any night of the week, one may sample big-band music for dancing, jazz from Dixie to progressive, rock and rhythm and blues, and folk singing at any of Manila's night clubs, discos and bistros. Manila has a big number of first class, air-conditioned movie houses that regularly show the latest films from the U.S. and Europe.

Some Useful Information

Government of the Philippines

On February 25, 1986 the 20-year strong-man rule of former Pres. Ferdinand E. Marcos in the Philippines came to an end. Pres. Corazon C. Aquino, widow of assassinated ex-Senator Benigno Aquino, was brought into power by People Power. Upon assumption of duty, she resolved to articulate the country's yearning for justice and economic progress by pure dedication and involvement. Since she came to power through peace, she is determined to govern by peace. Indeed her battlecry is peace and reconciliation.

Philippine Tourism

To rebuild the country from the economic ruins caused by

the past regime, the Aquino government is determined to attract more capital to the country through promotion of tourism. Proper consultations and strategies are now being devised by the Ministry of Tourism. Proper business incentives, developments and reforms are being studied for future implementation in order to attract foreign investments in the field of tourism.

There are several reasons why the Philippines is the right place for tourists. The islands are right in the middle of the Pacific basin and this freak of geography has been very advantageous to the country. To its north is the Asian mainland, to its south is Oceania. Being in such a strategic position, the Philippines is literally a melting pot of the Asian and Australian continents.

The climate in the Philippines is sub-tropic making it virtually a land of perpetual summers. The tranquil seas that ring its bays are generally calm and ideal for surfing, scuba-diving and water skiing.

Then there is the worldwide reputation of the Filipino as a very hospitable host. The warmth and cordiality a Filipino accords the foreign visitor is unequaled in the world.

The women in the Philippines are another reason why foreigners keep coming. The Filipino woman is one of the prettiest in the world—two of them having clinched the Miss Universe crown—Margie Moran in 1973 and Gloria Diaz in 1969, and three Miss International titles—Gemma Cruz in 1965, Aurora Pijuan in 1971 and Melanie Marquez in 1979.

Philippine National Symbols

Flag — The Philippine flag is composed of three parts: a white equilateral triangle on the left and two horizontal stripes, blue and red. It is unusual insofar as it indicates whether the country is at peace or at war: in times of peace, the blue is over the red and in times of war, the red over the blue. The eight rays of the Philippine sun, in the middle of the white triangle, represents the first eight provinces which revolted against the Spanish domination. The three stars at the triangle's corners indicate the three major groups of the Philippine islands: Luzon, Visayas and Mindanao. The triangle white with equal sides means equality. The sun symbolizes democracy. The field of red below the blue indicates courage while the field of blue above the red indicates truthfulness, peace and justice.

Dr. Jose Rizal is the national hero whose two novels, *Noli Me Tangere* and *El Filibusterismo*, opened the eyes of Filipinos and led to the fight for independence in 1896.

Maria Clara, the heroine in Rizal's novels, symbolizes the true Filipina, a model of modesty and grace.

The *sampaguita* is the national flower.

The *narra* is the national tree.

The *nipa hut* symbolizes the Filipino home where life is simple and love ties strong and fast.

The *pearl* symbolizes the Philippines itself; it is often called the "Pearl of the Orient Seas."

Anahaw is the national leaf.

The *mango* is the national fruit—the king of Philippine fruits. When ripe it has a luscious taste made more lovely by its heart-like shape.

The *lechon* symbolizes festivity, no food festival being considered complete without this suckling pig broiled to a golden brown.

The national fish is the *bangus*, a milky-white fish.

The *tinikling* is the national native dance unique in itself. Between the merry clicking together of bamboos, dancers jump in and out with rhythm and grace.

The *maya* is the national bird.

The *piña* is the national cloth woven out of pineapple plant fibers.

Tuba is the national drink—wine fermented from coconut water.

Sipa is the national game played by kicking back and forth over a net between two players a ball made of light native rattan.

The *kudyapi* is a national musical instrument—a sort of elongated guitar with only three strings.

The *rondalla* is a Philippine string ensemble played with native instruments such as the banduria, bajo, guitar, *laud*, octavina and picolo.

The *salakot* is the national hat made from nipa leaves. It is big and round and worn over the head with ease.

The *barong tagalog* is the national attire for men. It is originally woven from piña fiber.

The *balintawak* is the national female attire. It has butterfly sleeves and is named after the place where the first cry for national freedom was made.

National Seal: The Great Seal of the Republic of the Philippines — The Great Seal designed by Capt. Galo B. Ocampo, member and secretary of the Philippine Heraldry Committee was approved by Commonwealth Act No. 731, Congress of the Philippines on July 3, 1946. The Philippine history is reflected in the coat of arms of the Republic, from the eight-rayed Philippine Sun to the three five-pointed Stars which are one and inseparable. The point of honor in the center is occupied by the Philippine Sun Rayonnant while Luzon, Visayas and Mindanao are represented by the Three Stars which occupy the chief portion of the shield. The baldheaded American Eagle occupies the right side on a field of blue and the Lion Rampant occupies the left side on a field of red.

The National Anthem

Bayang magiliw, Perlas ng Silanganan
Alab ng puso sa dibdib mo'y buhay.
Lupang Hinirang, Duyan ka ng magiting
Sa manlulupig di ka pasisiil.

Sa dagat at bundok
Sa simoy at sa langit mong bughaw,
May dilag ang tula
At awit sa paglayang minamahal.

Ang kislap ng watawat mo'y
Tagumpay na nagniningning
Ang bituin at araw niya
Kailan pa ma'y di magdidilim.

Lupa ng araw, ng luwalhati't pagsinta,
Buhay ay langit sa piling mo;
Aming ligaya na pag may mang-aapi
Ang mamatay nang dahil sa iyo.

REFERENCE NOTES

[1]Lourdes V. Lapuz, *A Study of Psychopathology* (Quezon City: New Day Publishers, 1978), p. 226.

[2]Tito A. Mijares, "Philippine Population: Present and Future Prospects," *The Fookien Times Philippine Yearbook* (1983–84), pp. 274–277.

[3]Ibid.

[4]Jovita Varias-de Guzman and Rodolfo R. Varias, *Psychology of Filipinos* (Studies and Essays) (Manila: 1967), pp. 71–80.

[5]Rodolfo V. Gulang, *Philippine Medical Superstitions Told in Parables* (Lingayen, Pangasinan: Gumawid Press, 1960).

[6]S. P. Flores, *Aklat ng mga Panaginip at mga Kahulugan* (Manila: Philippine Book Company, 1958), pp. 95–97.

[7]Jaime Bulatao, S.J., *Split-Level Christianity* (Manila: Ateneo University Press, 1967), pp. 24–25.

[8]Frank Lynch and Mary R. Hollnsteiner, *The Filipino Family, Community and Nation*, IPC Papers. No. 12 (1978).

[9]Ceferino Z. Zaide, Jr., *Preparing for Responsible Parenthood* (Quezon City: National Book Store, 1973), p. 80.

[10]Dionisia R. de la Paz, "Preferences for Number and Sex of Children in the Philippines," *Population Forum*, vol. 1, no. 2 (August, 1975), p. 6.

[11]Varias-de Guzman, op. cit., pp. 131–132.

[12]Amparo Lardizabal and Felicitas Tensuan-Leogardo, *Readings on Philippine Culture and Social Life* (Caloocan City: Philippine Graphic Arts, Inc., 1980).

[13]Varias-de Guzman, op. cit.

¹⁴Clyde Kluckholm and Henry A. Murray, "Personality Formation: The Determinants," *Personality in Nature, Society and Culture* (New York: Knopf, 1956), p. 53.

¹⁵F. Landa Jocano, "Management and Culture: A Normative Approach," A Paper read during the Personnel Management Association of the Philippines' Convention, Baguio City, 1981.

¹⁶George M. Guthrie and Pepita Jimenez Jacobs, *Child Rearing and Personality Development in the Philippines* (Manila: Bookmark, Inc., 1967).

¹⁷Jocano, op. cit., p. 3.   ¹⁸Ibid., p. 12.

¹⁹Tomas D. Andres, *Management by Filipino Values* (Quezon City: New Day Publishers, 1985), pp. 159–160.

²⁰Jaime Bulatao, S.J., "Relevance in Philippine Psychology," PAP Presidential Address, October, 1979.

²¹Zaide, op. cit., p. 50.

²²Tomas D. Andres et al., *Sex Education and Family Planning for Filipinos* (Quezon City: Ken Incorporated, 1974).

²³Ibid., pp. 65–66.

²⁴United States Navy, *Overseas Diplomacy* (Washington, D.C.: Government Printing Office, 1973).

²⁵JoAnn Craig, *Culture Shock!* (Singapore: Times Books International, 1979), pp. 159–169.

²⁶Model provided by Clyde and Florence Kluckholm and Frederick Strodtbeck.

²⁷Adapted from "Living and Working in Saudi Arabia," Mimeographed Manual given during a three-day Orientation Program for Dravo employees and their spouses. Dravo Personnel Staff.

²⁸Seymour H. Fersh, "Semantics and the Study of Culture," a Handout distributed during an English Seminar. Met. Manila, Lourdes School, 1973.

²⁹Philip Harris, "The Unhappy World of the Expatriate," *International Management*, vol. 34, no. 7 (July, 1979), pp. 49–50.

³⁰Fr. Miguel Ma. Valera, "New Dimensions in Human Resource Management," Address delivered during the 18th National Conference of the Personnel Management Ass. of the Phil. in Baguio City, Oct. 23, 1981.

³¹K. P. Clements, "The Expatriate as a Stranger," *The Voice* (University of Hong Kong Students Union, March, 1973).

³²Albert D. Justiniano, "Culture Shock and How to Overcome It," A Paper in Human Resource Management II Course. Makati: Ateneo Graduate School of Business, September 17, 1985.

BIBLIOGRAPHY

A. BOOKS

Agoncillo, Teodoro A. *Philippine History.* Manila: Inang Wika Publishing Co., 1962.

Andres, Tomas Quintin, Josefina Gaerlan and Delia Limpingco. *Sex Education and Family Planning for Filipinos.* Quezon City: Ken, Inc., 1974.

Anima, Nid. *Courtship and Marriage Practices Among Philippine Tribes.* Quezon City: Omar Publications, 1975.

Araneta, Francisco, S.J. *Values and Institutions for Socio-Economic Reforms.* Manila: Araneta University, 1975.

Batacan, Delfin Fl. *Looking at Ourselves.* Manila: Philaw Publishing, 1956.

Bello, Walden F. and Maria Clara Roldan. *Modernization: Its Impact in the Philippines.* IPC Papers No. 4, 1967.

Benitez, Conrado. *Philippine Social Life and Progress.* Boston: Ginn and Company, 1937.

Beyer, Otley H. and Jaime C. de Veyra. *Philippine Saga.* Third Edition. Manila, Philippines: Capitol Publishing House, Inc., 1952.

Bulatao, Jaime, S.J. *Split-Level Christianity.* Quezon City: Ateneo de Manila University Press, 1966.

Capino, Diosdada G. *Philippine Social Life.* Manila, 1951.

Caroll, John J. *Changing Patterns of Social Structures in the Philippines.* Quezon City: Ateneo de Manila University Press, 1968.

_____. *Philippine Institutions.* Manila: Solidaridad Publishing House, 1970.

Carrion, J. Antonio. *An Introduction to Marketing Imperatives.* Manila: National Book Store, Inc., 1971.

_____. *Salesmanship Imperatives.* Manila: University of the East, Department of Marketing, Management, Communications and Behavioral Science, 1974.

Casino, Eric. *Folk Islam in the Life Cycle of the Jama Mapun.* Manila: Solidaridad Publishing House, 1968.

_____. *Philippine Culture and the Filipino Intellectuals.*

Castelo, Lea T. *This Is the Philippines.* Quezon City: Melencio M. Castelo Publisher, 1977.

China Airlines. *Travel Guide.* 1974.

Constantino, Renato. *The Filipino Elite.* Quezon City: Malaya Books, Inc., 1967.

_____. *The Miseducation of the Filipino.* Quezon City: Malaya Books, Inc., 1966.

Cordero, Felicidad V. and Isabel S. Panopio. *General Sociology.* Quezon City: Ken, Inc., 1971.

Coronel, Maria Delia. *Stories and Legends from Filipino Folklore.* Philippines: University of Santo Tomas Press, 1967.

Costa, Horacio de la, S.J. *Asia and the Philippines.* Manila: Solidaridad Publishing House, 1967.

Craig, Austin and Conrado Benitez. *The Philippine Progress Prior to 1898-1916.*

_____. *Former Philippines Through Foreign Eye.*

Craig, JoAnn. *Culture Shock!* Singapore: Times Books International, 1979.

Enriquez, Virgilio G. *Filipino Psychology in the Third World.* 1977.

Espiritu, Socorro and Chester Hunt. *Social Foundations of Community Development.* Manila: R. M. Garcia Publishing House, 1964.

Fernandez, Alejandro M. *International Law in Philippine Relations: 1898-1946.* 1971.

Flores, S. P. *Aklat ng mga Panaginip at mga Kahulugan.* Manila: Philippine Book Company, 1958.

Gonzalez, Anna Miren and Mary Racelis Hollnsteiner. *Filipino Women as Partners of Men in Progress and Development.* Quezon City: PSSC, 1976.

Gorospe, Vitaliano, S.J. *Christian Renewal of Filipino Values.* Quezon City: Ateneo de Manila University Press.

_____. *Responsible Parenthood in the Philippines.* Manila: Ateneo de Manila Publications, 1970.

Gowing, Peter G. and William Henry Scott. *Acculturation in the Philippines.* Quezon City: New Day Publishers, 1971.

_____. *Mandate in Moroland.* Quezon City: New Day Publishers, 1977.

176

_____. *The Muslim Filipinos*. Manila: Solidaridad Publishing House, 1974.

Guerrero-Nakpil, Carmen. *Filipino Cultural Roots and Foreign Influences*. Davao City: U.S. Information Service, 1970.

Gulang, Rodolfo V. *Philippine Medical Superstitions Told in Parables*. Lingayen, Pangasinan: Gumawid Press, 1960.

Guthrie, George M. and Pepita J. Jacobs. *Child Rearing and Personality Development in the Philippines*. Manila: PNS Press, 1967.

_____. *The Filipino Child and Philippine Society*. Manila: PNS Press, 1961.

_____. *The Psychology of Modernization in the Rural Philippines* (IPC Paper No. 8), Quezon City: Ateneo de Manila University Press, 1971.

_____. *Six Perspectives on the Philippines*. Manila: Bookmark, 1971.

Hollnsteiner, Mary. *Dynamics of Power in a Philippine Municipality*. Quezon City: PSSC, 1963.

Hunt, Chester L. et al. *Sociology in the Philippine Setting*. Manila: Alemar's, 1954.

_____. *Sociology in the Philippine Setting*. U.S.A.: Pheonix Publishing House, 1963.

Institute of International Education. *Practical Guide for Foreign Visitors*. U.S.A., 1976.

Jacoby, Erich H. *Agrarian Unrest in Southeast Asia*. New York: Columbia University Press, 1959.

Jenks, Albert. *Bontoc Igorot*. Manila: Philippine Printing Press, 1905.

Jocano, F. Landa. *Philippine Prehistory: An Anthropological Overview of the Beginnings of Filipino Society and Culture*. Quezon City: University of the Philippines Press, 1975.

Kassarjian, J. B. M. and Robert A. Stringer, Jr. *The Management of Men*. Manila: Molina's Copier Center, 1970.

Lardizabal, Amparo S. and Felicitas Tensuan-Leogardo. *Readings on Philippine Culture and Social Life*. Caloocan City: Philippine Graphic Arts, Inc., 1980.

Laurel, Jose P. *Forces That Make a Nation Great*. Manila: National Teachers College Press, 1948.

Laviña, Francisco Bernardo. *Papers in Mindanao Ethnography, Data Paper No. 1*. Marawi City, Philippines: University Research Center, MSU, 1979.

Liao, Shubert S. C. *Chinese Participation in Philippine Culture and Economy*. N.p. 1964 as cited in Leonardo N. Mercado's *Elements of Filipino Philosophy*. Tacloban City: Divine Word University Publication.

Lynch, Frank, S.J. *Social Acceptance Reconsidered.* Quezon City: Institute of Philippine Culture. Ateneo de Manila University, 1973.

_____. *Understanding the Philippines and America: A Study of Cultural Themes.* Quezon City: Institute of Philippine Culture, Ateneo de Manila University, 1968.

_____ and Alfonso de Guzman, II. *Four Readings on Philippine Values.* Quezon City: IPC Papers No. 2, 1973.

_____ and Mary R. Hollnsteiner. *The Filipino Family, Community and Nation.* IPC Papers No. 12, 1978.

Madale, Abdullah T. *The Remarkable Maranaws.* Quezon City: Omar Publications, 1976.

Marcos, Ferdinand E. *A Dialogue with My People.* Manila: Department of Public Information, 1971.

_____. *Revolution From the Center.* Hong Kong: Raya Books, 1978.

Martinez-Esquillo, Natividad. *Conjugal Interaction and Fertility Behavior Among the Filipino Urban Working Class.* 1976.

Mayuga, Sylvia and Alfred Yuson et al. *Philippines.* Hong Kong: APA Productions, 1980.

Mercado, Leonardo N. *Elements of Filipino Philosophy.* Tacloban City: Divine Word University Publications, 1976.

_____. *Filipino Religious Psychology.* Tacloban City: Divine Word University Publications, 1977.

Ministry of Tourism. *Come to Our Island World Philippines.* Manila, Philippines, 1975.

_____. *Philippine Guidebook.* Manila, Philippines, 1975.

_____. *Primer on the Philippines.* Manila, Philippines, 1975.

Molina, Antonio M. *The Philippines Through the Centuries.* Manila: University of Santo Tomas Cooperative, 1968.

Montemayor, Jeremias U. *Philippine Socio-Economic Problems.* Manila: Rex Book Store, 1962.

Montiel, Cristina and Mary R. Hollnsteiner. *The Filipino Woman: Her Role and Status in Philippine Society.* 1976.

Nabayra, Kurais II. *Papers in Mindanao Ethnography. Data Paper No. 2.* Marawi City, Philippines: University Research Center, MSU, 1979.

Nelson, Raymund. *The Philippines.* London: Thames and Hudson, 1968.

Osias, Camilo. *The Filipino Way of Life.* Boston: Ginn and Company, 1940.

Office of Civil Relations, Philippine Army. *Towards the Restructuring of Filipino Values.* 1970.

Philippine Convention Bureau. *Manila.* Philippines, 1975.

Philippine Tourism Authority. *A Guide for Tourism Investors in the Philippines.* Philippines, 1975.

_____. *The Philippine Tourism Authority and You.* Philippines, 1975.

Post, Elizabeth L. *Emily Post's Pocket Book of Etiquette.* New York: Pocket Books, 1967.

Quisumbing, Lourdes. *Marriage Customs in Rural Cebu.* Cebu City: San Carlos Publications, 1974.

Rixhon, Gerard. *Sulu Studies 2 and 3.* Jolo: Notre Dame of Jolo College, 1974.

Saber, Mamitua and Abdullah T. Madale. *The Maranao.* Manila: Solidaridad Publishing House, 1975.

SGV and Co. *Doing Business in the Philippines.* Makati, 1975.

Sixth Annual Seminar for Student Leaders. *The Philippine-American Relationship.* Philippines: U.S. Information Service, 1974.

Tagle, Ramon, Jr. *Towards a Responsible Parenthood and Family Life.* Philippines: S.C.C. Development and Research Foundation, 1974.

United States Navy. *Guidelines for United States Navy Overseas Diplomacy.* Washington, D.C.: Government Printing Office, 1973.

University of the Philippines Population Institute. *Philippine Population Profiles, Prospects and Problems.* Quezon City: University of the Philippines Press, 1970.

Varias-de Guzman, Jovita and Rodolfo R. Varias. *Psychology of Filipinos.* Manila, Philippines, 1967.

Varias. Rodolfo R. *Lectures in Psychiatry.* Manila, Philippines, 1970.

Victoriano, Herminia A. *Pilipinism.* Quezon City: Manlapaz Publishing Co., 1969.

Zaide, Ceferino A. Jr. *Preparing for Responsible Parenthood.* Quezon City: National Book Store, Inc., 1973.

Zaide, Gregorio F. *History of the Filipino People.* Manila: The Modern Book Co., 1964.

_____. *Philippine Political and Cultural History.* Manila: Philippine Education Company, 1957.

Zshornack, Emma J. et al. *Philippine Popular Apologetics.* Manila: University of Santo Tomas Cooperative, 1962.

B. ARTICLES

Andres, Tomas Quintin D. "The Filipino Philosophy of Values," *Personnel Management Association of the Philippines Newsletter* (March, 1980).

_____. "Who Is the Filipino?" *Personnel Management Association of the Philippines Newsletter* (January, 1980).

Anima, Nid. "Marriage in Ilocandia," *Woman's Home Companion* (June 14, 1973), pp. 38-39.

Arboleda, A. R. Jr. "Christmas, Holy Week and the Filipino Christian," *Homelife*, vol. XXVI, no. 12 (December, 1980), pp. 14-17.

Arjona, Adoracion. "The Ningas-Kugon and the Mañana Habit," *Unitas*, vol. 37 (1965).

Batara, Armando P. "Euphemisms for 'Insufficiency of Funds' Hurt Business," *Getty News* (1978).

Bulatao, Jaime L., S.J. "Changing Social Values," *Philippine Studies*, vol. 10, no. 2 (April, 1962).

_____. "Hiya," *Philippine Studies*, vol. 12, no. 3 (1964).

_____. "The Hiya System on Filipino Culture," *The Philippine Educational Forum*, vol. 14 (1965).

_____. "Personal Preferences of Filipino Students," *Philippine Sociological Review* (July-October, 1970).

_____. "Philippine Values I: The Manileños Mainsprings," *Philippine Studies*, vol. 10 (January 1962), pp. 32-44.

_____. "Relevance on Philippine Psychology," PAP Presidential Address (October 11-13, 1979).

_____. "Value Orientation of the Filipino Consumer," *Marketing Horizons*, vol. 3 (January, 1964).

Catarroja, Sebastian, "Virtues and Vices of the Filipino Family," *Philippine Panorama*, vol. 1, no. 19 (December 8, 1972), pp. 6-10.

Cordero-Fernando, Gilda. "Coping with the Undomesticated Filipino Husband or No Left Turn," *Woman's Home Companion* (April 19, 1973), pp. 6-9.

Dagdayan, Celia B. "Female Circumcision," *Women's Home Companion* (January 25, 1973), pp. 3-4.

De la Paz, Dionisia R. "Preferences for Number and Sex of Children in the Philippines," *Population Forum*, vol. 1, no. 2 (August, 1975), pp. 8-10.

De la Torre, Visitacion R. "The Filipino as Lover," *Philippine Panorama* (February 9, 1975).

Espino, Federico Licsi Jr. "How Americanized Are the Young?," *Mod*, vol. 7, no. 202 (July 4, 1975), pp. 8-10.

Fabian, Mac A. "The Filipino Peasant's Culture of Repression," *The Sunday Times Magazine* (February 7, 1971), pp. 6-7.

Fernandez, Doreen G. "The Filipino Christmas Table," *Asian Catholic Digest*, vol. no. 1 (December, 1980), pp. 37-44.

_____. "The Rites That Makes Up a Filipino Christmas," *Pagsulong*, vol. 6, no. 12 (December, 1979), p 20.

Fernando, Deogracias. "The Tyranny of 'Awa' in Personnel Management," *PMAP Newsletter* (March–April, 1975), pp. 3–5.

Flores, Jimmy. "A Study in Suicide: The Filipino as a Fatalist," *The Sunday Times Magazine* (June 23, 1968), pp. 44–46.

Fox, Robert B. "Ancient Filipino Communities," *Filipino Cultural Heritage*. Manila: Philippine Women's University (1966).

_____. "The Filipino Concept of Self-Esteem," *Area Handbook on the Philippines*. Chicago: Human Relations *Area Files* (1956).

_____. "The Pinatubo Negritoes: Their Useful Plants Material Culture," *Philippine Journal of Science* (1954), p. 188.

Franco, Ernesto A. "Management, Pinoy Style," *HR Magazine* (May, 1979), pp. 21–24.

Guerrero-Nakpil Carmen. "Consensus of One: Will Success Spoil the Filipino?," *The Sunday Times Magazine* (September 21, 1969), pp. 20–21.

_____. "Filipinos Are (W)ild Drinkers," *The Sunday Times Magazine* (October 31, 1971), pp. 15–16.

_____. "The Present Imperfect of the English Language in the Third Largest English-Speaking Country," *Expressweek* (September 6, 1973), pp. 14–15.

_____. "A Question of Indentity," *The Sunday Times Magazine* (April 9, 1972), pp. 11–12.

_____. "Why Filipinos Believe in Luck," *The Sunday Times Magazine* (December 12, 1971), pp. 11–12.

Hollnsteiner, Mary R. "Reciprocity as a Filipino Value, Society, Culture and the Filipino," *IPC* no. 2 (1976).

_____. "Social Control and the Filipino Personality," *PRS* vol. 2, nos. 3 and 4 (1963).

Hunt, Chester L. "Changing Social Patterns in the Philippines," *Silliman Journal* (First Quarter, 1962), pp. 32–43.

Jocano, F. Landa. "Filipino Social Structure and Value System," *Filipino Cultural Heritage*. Manila: Philippine Women's University, 1966.

_____ and P. Mendez. "The Filipino Family in Its Rural and Urban Orientation," Two Core Studies, Manila Research and Development Center, Centro Escolar University, 1974.

Justiniane, Albert D. "Culture Shock and How to Overcome It," (a paper in Human Resource Management II Course), Makati: Ateneo Graduate School of Business, September 17, 1985.

Largoza, Conchita H. "When Its Best to Say 'No.' Assertiveness Training for

Filipinos," *Personnel Management Association of the Philippines Newsletter* (November, 1980), pp. 10–11.

Lopez, Julian. "The Filipino as a Planner," A Research Paper on Management, University of the Philippines (1968).

Lynch, Frank. "Philippine Values II: Social Acceptance," *Philippine Studies*, vol. 10 (January, 1962), pp. 82–99.

Madale, Abdullah T. "Education for Filipino Muslims," *Philippine Panorama* (July 21, 1974), pp. 17–18.

Mercado, Monina A. "Fiestas Are Forever."

_____. "Honoring San Isidro," *The Sunday Times Magazine* (May 21, 1972), pp. 26–27.

Miranda, Augusto. "Wedding Traditions in the Philippines," *Woman's Home Companion* (June 11, 1980), pp. 10–11.

Morales, Rosalina. *Ugaling Pilipino* (unpublished manuscript).

Olanio, Yolanda L. "The Filipino Women Today: Some Vital Statistics," *HR Magazine* (September, 1979), pp. 24–25.

Panizo, Alfredo, O.P. "The Negritoes of Aetas," *UNITAS* 40.1: 67–69 (March, 1967).

Poblador, Arce. "Formal Organizations in the Philippines," *Philippine Studies*, vol. 25 (First Quarter, 1977).

Quisumbing, Lourdes R. "Philippine Cultural Values and Development," (unpublished manuscript).

Ramirez, Mina. "The Filipino Family, Philippine Institutions and the Value System," (unpublished material).

Rimon, Jose G. II. "Reviving Folk Media," *Population Forum*, vol. 1, no. 4 (October, 1975), pp. 2–5.

Romero, L. Z. "Campus Survey: The Filipino College Student Talks on Love and Marriage," *Mod Filipina*, vol. 7, no. 221 (November 14, 1975), pp. 14–15.

Santiago, Cynthia U. "The Filipino Manager," *HR Magazine* (May, 1979), pp. 15–19.

Senden, Francis. "Positive Aspects of Philippine Values," (unpublished material).

Soria, Estanislao A. "Toward Identifying the Values and Positivising the Negatives," (unpublished material).

_____. "Toward Identifying Filipino Values: A Preliminary Report of the Institute of Mass Communication," University of the Philippines, Quezon City.

Tanjuatco, Edgardo. "Restructuring the Philippine Value System," (unpublished material).

Tulio, Artemio L. "Negritoes in the Province of Capiz," *Negrito-Aeta Paper No. 77,* Manila: 1916.

Tupas, Rodolfo G. "Why Filipino Women Are Pampered," *Expressweek* (September 6, 1973), pp. 11-12.

Valencia, Teodoro F. "The Compadre System," *Expressweek* (September 6, 1973).

_____. "The Image of the Filipino Through Foreign Eyes," *Expressweek* (June 27, 1974).

Varias, Rodolfo. "Psychiatry and the Filipino Personality," *Philippine Sociological Review* (July–October, 1973).

Ventura, Sylvia Mendez. "Why the Filipino Should Walk Proud," *Woman's Home Companion* (August 2, 1973), pp. 15-17.

Villegas, Bernardo M. and Carlos A. Abola. "Towards a More Productive Filipino Worker," Center for Research and Communication (May, 1974).

Villote, Fr. Ben J. "The Filipino as Contemplative," *Philippine Panorama* (March 16, 1975), pp. 13-14.

(Dr. Tomas Andres . . .)

Bank and the National Manpower and Youth Council, lecturer of the Central Bank Institute, the University of Life, International Management Executive Center and a doctoral professor at the Eulogio "Amang" Rodriguez Institute of Science and Technology. Dr. Andres is the editor-in-chief of *The Philippine Values Digest,* the first and only Filipino journal on Philippine values education.

*****

(Mrs. Pilar Andres . . .)

Magsaysay School of Medicine.

Mrs. Andres who is pursuing her master's degree in guidance and counseling at the Eulogio "Amang" Rodriguez Institute of Science and Technology, has had several years' experience in successful teaching and counseling work. She has gone into research work in the areas of education, counseling and psychology. She is presently a columnist in the *Philippine Values Digest* and vice president for business development of the Values and Technologies Management Centre.